D0880936

Monarchs and Mercenaries

Monarchs and Mercenaries

A Reappraisal of the Importance of
Knight Service in Norman
and Early Angevin England

by John Schlight

USAF Academy

CBS\UB

Published by the Conference on British Studies
at the University of Bridgeport, Connecticut

© 1968 BY THE UNIVERSITY OF BRIDGEPORT
LIBRARY OF CONGRESS CATALOG CARD NUMBER: 68-15335
MANUFACTURED IN THE UNITED STATES OF AMERICA

Produced and Distributed by New York University Press

To Ellen

Preface

Studies in British History and Culture, a joint venture of the
Conference on British Studies and the University of Bridgeport,
was founded in January, 1965. The first round of manuscript competition was announced at the Fall 1965 Conference meeting. No
one expected then that more than forty manuscripts would be sub-
mitted in the next eighteen months.

From the screening of many readers and editors, two manuscripts have emerged as winners in the first phase of competition.
John Schlight's *Monarchs & Mercenaries* is the first of these to
be published. Professor Schlight's work, which inaugurates this
Monograph Series, meets many of the ideals laid down for the
Series by the editors and other Conference officials who conceived
it. These ideals include vigorous research, original interpretation,
literary grace, and the prospect of interest among scholars in several
fields. The editors were especially seeking works which would
challenge traditional viewpoints. Professor Schlight's volume ad-
mirably fulfills this last ideal. He assembles impressive evidence to
support his thesis that mercenary troops rather than knights-on-
horseback constituted a dominant institution in feudal society.

Studies in British History and Culture generally, and this first
monograph in particular, ought to be regarded as a tribute to
Walter Love, the first Managing Editor, who died tragically after
laying the foundation for the Series. Professor Love negotiated the
production arrangement with the New York University Press,
solicited and screened the initial large group of manuscripts, and
handled innumerable business matters prerequisite to publishing this
first book. It is our hope that *Studies in British History and Culture*
will come to be regarded as a viable memorial to his energy, imagination, and devotion.

Stephen Graubard
Leland Miles
Senior Editors

ACKNOWLEDGEMENT

The preceding work owes a great debt to a large number of persons, known and unknown, spanning the last nine centuries. Chroniclers, as well as recorders of official political and financial documents, have provided us with the fundamental materials from which to reconstruct their story. While space limitations have prevented me from thanking, in fullsome footnotes, each of these scribes individually, I take here the opportunity to do so collectively.

Thanks is also due to the last several generations of historians who have unveiled many of the intricacies of medieval institutions. Foremost among them is Joseph R. Strayer of Princeton University who has had the largest and most direct influence upon me and to whom I owe the greatest debt. I also wish to thank Warren Hollister and Norman Cantor who with kindness and professionalism set aside their other tasks to read and comment upon my original manuscript.

An equal share of gratitude goes out to my wife, Ellen, who often and willingly postponed her love-affair with the present that I might continue mine with the past.

J. S.

Contents

Preface   *vii*

I   Mercenaries and Historians   3

II   Who Were the Mercenaries?   14

III   William I and His Sons   26

IV   King Stephen   40

V   Henry Plantagenet   53

VI   Conclusion   72

     Appendix A: Military Campaigns and Sieges (1066–1189)   77

     Appendix B: The Fragmentation of Knights' Fees (1135–1166)   80

     Appendix C: Value in Pounds of the Land Held by the Ten Leading Companions of William the Conqueror   82

     Appendix D: Scutage Totals for the Reign of Henry II (1154–1189)   84

     Appendix E: Annual Expenditures for Castle Soldiers and Castle Construction (1158–1189)   85

     Notes   88

     Bibliography   91

     Index   99

STUDIES IN BRITISH HISTORY AND CULTURE

VOLUME I

STUDIES IN BRITISH HISTORY AND CULTURE

VOLUME I

CHAPTER I

Mercenaries and Historians

OF all the products of man's mind none is more complex than the institutions he creates to serve and give purpose to his society. This complexity is attributable to the fact that the needs of any society are constantly changing thereby requiring continual modification of the institutions devised to satisfy them. As hard as it is to describe a living institution at any given moment in history, it is infinitely more difficult to retrace the steps whereby an institution developed from a seminal idea to a well organized social structure. The further back in history one goes the more difficult becomes the task of uncovering the genesis of institutions. Scarcity of records is part of the problem. But a more subtle obstacle lies in the fact that by the time an idea has become institutionalized and accepted as an instrument of society the need which evoked it has often passed or been satisfied elsewhere. Often during this period of gestation the spotlight is focused on some other institution, even one directly antithetical to the one under examination. Such, for example, is the case with the institution of mercenaries and their use in European armies. This military institution became of documented importance only in the fifteenth and sixteenth centuries. Before that time feudalism and the mounted knight received the bulk of attention in literature. Nevertheless, during the very period of the supposed predominance of the feudal warrior new needs were rendering the knight obsolete and demanding the use of hired soldiers. It is to this earlier period that the historian must turn if he is to discover how and why mercenaries became a vital force in European military and social history.

Not all societies possess the same degree of flexibility. Few generations in the history of the West have played out their institutional role against a background fluid enough to merit the title of *tabula rasa*. Such was surely the context within which the American founding fathers created our form of government. The choices open to them upon the rejection of English political institutions ranged across the entire spectrum of political forms. The same was true of the French who replaced their feudal forms with republican ones at the close of the eighteenth century. The American and French experience was paralleled in many ways by the Russians who cleared the board in the twentieth century and began anew. Although in each of these instances the opportunity for deep-seated change was provided by a revolutionary removal of earlier forms, it is not only within such a radical context that these same results can be achieved. There have been other periods in European history during which similarly basic institutional changes have occurred, although with less rapidity and drama. The twelfth century was one of them.

An age that is institutionally fluid is one in which the leaders of society and those primarily responsible for creating institutions for that society are largely unrestrained in their choice of institutions by already existing forms. It is a critical period when a crossroad has been reached and a selection of institutional forms must be made. Despite subsequent alteration the original forms become an integral part of the state and harden with time. The key element in this fluidity is the freedom of choice whereby a ruler can base his decisions on suitability rather than tradition.

Europe in the late eleventh and twelfth centuries was institutionally fluid. Historians have traced to this period the origins of a number of institutions which have since become identified with western culture. The university, capitalism, certain forms of local government, the Exchequer, the income tax and the jury system had their roots in these centuries. But more important than the story of the actual development of these institutions is the fact that even as late as the twelfth century they could still have grown in entirely different directions. For example, there was a great need at that time for the Church to organize and control the mountain of knowledge that was entering Europe from the south and east in order to digest and disseminate it. While the eleventh century bequeathed this need to the twelfth it did not dictate the nature of the institution which was to satisfy it. The university which developed in answer to this need was born of the requirements of the moment and its forms reflected these rather than a slavish imitation of the earlier monastic and cathedral schools.

The same may be said of the nascent capitalism of the twelfth century which, while satisfying a need born of the eleventh-century revival of trade and commerce, in no way inherited its form from the immediately pre-existing economy. The institutions devised to facilitate the accumulation of capital, such as banking and investment organizations, displayed little if any continuity with the earlier period. Even those twelfth-century institutions which bear traces of earlier forms, such as Gothic architecture, local government, and the jury system, were essentially responses to present needs and contained more of the new than of the old. In each case the resultant form was one of several possible choices, and it was this flexibility in institutional development that made the period such a critical and at the same time exciting one.

The case of England during this period was at once unique and controversial. Its seizure by the Normans has injected into the institutional argument there an element missing from discussions about other European areas. Rather than aiding in the solution of the institutional issue, William the Conqueror's successful invasion in 1066 has complicated it and led to two widely divergent interpretations. One view of the results of the Norman Conquest pictures the changes wrought by this event as no less sudden nor substantial than those of the later American, French and Russian revolutions. Others fail to see any basic alteration of English institutions as a result of 1066. The Norman Conquest is thus seen by one group as the catalyst of institutional change and by the other as the furnace within which pre-Conquest institutions were tried and found stable. The former view has dominated the field for the past two generations. The latter interpretation was favored in the nineteenth century and is presently enjoying a revival. This debate has been fruitful in many ways. Most directly it has shed light upon medieval English society, military institutions and financial organization. Less direct, but of no less importance, are the implications it holds for British institutional and social development in later centuries. It is worth the time to pause for an examination of the key elements of the controversy for therein lie the seeds of the present discussion of mercenaries.

Students of medieval England in the nineteenth century preferred to place the Norman Conquest in the much larger context of earlier and, to their way of thinking, more portentous invasions which shook the island—that of the Angles and Saxons and those of the Danes. By comparison the Norman invasion appeared minor. Except for the introduction of a relatively small group of foreigners into the upper levels of society, they saw no substantial alteration of Anglo-Saxon institutions. This manner of viewing things changed suddenly at the dawn of the twentieth century. Inspired by the drastic revisionism of John Horace Round in the 1890's, the majority of the scholars of the past 70 years have followed his lead by picturing the Conquest as the most revolutionary episode in English history. In his original thesis Round, by his own admission, focused attention on but one of several possible elements, namely knight-service, and those who have followed him, both as supporters and adversaries, have tended to do the same.[1] For this reason the entire discussion has at times been criticized as myopic. These criticisms have not been entirely fair, for the microcosmic character of the institution of knight-service causes any discussion of it to broaden out to include the supposedly slighted areas.

Pre-Roundian historians defined English feudalism much the same as they did continental feudalism. Since little distinction was made between the island and mainland varieties it followed that, for them, an invasion from the continent, such as that of 1066, brought little that was new. In order to justify his cataclysmic theory of the Norman Conquest, according to which the Normans introduced substantial changes in Anglo-Saxon institutions, Round had to endow post-Conquest England with a distinctive quality that could set it apart from the pre-Conquest system. This he thought he found in knight-service, an arrangement whereby land was held in return for an annual military commitment. According to his now generally accepted theory feudalism, clothed in the garb of this knight-service, was introduced into England around the year 1070 when William first placed quotas for knight-service upon his more important followers, the tenants-in-chief. Although there is no direct evidence for this laying on of quotas, Round has reconstructed it from circumstantial evidence. By what method the tenants-in-chief met their quotas, continues the theory, was of no concern to the king, so long as the barons appeared when called accompanied by the required number of qualified fighting men. In other words, the working out of the system below the level of tenants-in-chief was "a mere detail," not of great importance to the development of English feudalism. Nevertheless, this second step, called "subinfeudation," is considered just as much an innovation of the Conqueror as the immediate assessments on the upper level. Despite the secondary role of subinfeudation it, together with the royal quotas, constitutes the revolution of William. Such is the essence of the prevailing view.

There has been a rising crescendo of dissent from this interpretation. One group of critics accepts the secondary role assigned to subinfeudation but disagrees with the "quota" part of the theory. The main argument of these historians is to the effect that the quotas found existing in the 1070's were not newly created but had had a long history in England dating back to Anglo-Saxon times. By pointing to this continuity these modern-day revisionists hope to modify the revolutionary aspects of the prevailing interpretation and reinstate the idea of stability so dear to nineteenth-century scholars. The second group of critics tends to ignore the question of quotas and to concentrate on subinfeudation. It goes one step further than the first group by extending continuity forward in time past the early-established quotas on down to the individual knight's fee. This is done by building a bridge between the post-Conquest enfeoffed knight and the pre-Conquest thegn. By so doing this latter group has caused the argument to come full cycle, for Round's original theory was launched against this very point of continuity.

Both anti-Roundian schools, however, accept one basic assumption of their common rival. It makes no difference whether they consider subinfeudation "a mere detail" or an integral part of feudalism, they all seem to agree that within a century of the invasion the system of knight-service had filtered down so effectively to the lowest feudal level through subinfeudation that a call from the king for military aid brought on the run—or rather on the trot —knights of all degrees anxious to fulfill the martial responsibilities they assumed with their fiefs. Nowhere amidst this swirl of controversy have the two basic assumptions of the relative unimportance of subinfeudation and the existence of effective knight-service in twelfth-century England been systematically tested, although the need for such a trial has been expressed.[2]

This theory of the two-stage development of feudalism needs closer examination for it is central to the whole question. For if the outline of the system was indeed introduced shortly after the Conquest through an assessment of quotas, all that remained for the twelfth century to do was to develop this institution along the lines of the preconceived form. That century would thereby lose the institutional elasticity so evident in other areas. No room would be left for chance or for the possibility that a shift in needs might have taken place after the initial plan had been devised. There is strong evidence, however, that the quota arrangement remained only the ideal on paper and that the realities of military recruitment were quite different. It is not unheard of in history that the gap between what the official record says and what actually exists is more often than not a yawning one. One need only examine, for example, the discrepancy between the post-Versailles German *armée de métier* which existed on paper and its true nature as the nucleus of Hitler's war machine. A contemporary example is seen in the noticeable dearth of horses in the modern American cavalry division. The official record seems to have fooled Round and most of his successors and deflected them away from an examination of what actually existed in medieval armies. There is substantial evidence to suggest that the post-Conquest English military organization bore a minimal resemblance to the plans laid out for it, and that unforeseen factors intervened to cause this shift in direction.

Round's argument which downgrades subinfeudation as a "matter of secondary importance" is a forced one, developed, it would seem, as the way out of a dilemma. The corner into which he had worked himself was that of trying to preserve the revolutionary nature of the introduction of feudalism into England in the face of indisputable evidence that subinfeudation was a gradual process, still incomplete even in 1166. Unable to change the facts, he was forced to minimize their importance. This he did by locating the essential feudal element in that area which appeared to have come to England with a revolutionary rush, namely the quotas placed on the tenants-in-chief. There is no reason, however, why this interpretation, devised as a way out of a dilemma, should be elevated to the rank of a positive principle. If in no other way, it is apparent that quantitatively at least subinfeudation was certainly as important to feudalism as the original assessment of royal quotas. According to Round's own figures for 1166 there were 116 tenants-in-chief who were responsible for producing 2924 fighting men. To restrict feudalism to conditions affecting only the upper four percent of those ordinarily included in the feudal structure and to relegate the remaining ninety-six percent to a secondary and subsidiary position is unacceptable. An honest discussion of feudalism must include with equal pertinence all groups within the system. To maintain that the system of royal quotas was "the essential feature we have to keep in view" is, in effect, to deny that feudalism ever existed in England outside a mere handful of barons, since this statement neglects almost entirely those who, theoretically at least, filled the ranks of the so-called feudal array.

Round's second assumption was to the effect that subinfeudation was virtually complete by 1166 and was an effective system to provide warriors for royal and baronial wars. It is true that a royal inventory of knights' fees taken in that year, called the *Cartae Baronum*, indicates that the 116 tenants-in-chief mentioned above did subdivide their land in such a way as to expect the service of 2924 knights. But what is in no way indicated by these returns is the nature of this service—whether it was military, financial, judicial, or administrative. This could well be another instance of the official record in conflict with the actual composition of the army. It has been assumed almost universally among historians that knight-service meant actual service in the army. The "feudal array" which gallops through the pages of these authors exists only as a result of this assumption.

But this point is far too important to be entrusted to assumptions. We must look at what was, not at what should have been. A needed corrective is applied to the usual picture of a "feudal array" when we turn from the "official muster-roll" of 1166 and search through contemporary financial, administrative and narrative sources. What we find there is that feudal warriors, when they were present on medieval battlegrounds, were seldom alone. Almost invariably they were accompanied by hired, non-feudal soldiers who, if not always numerically superior, often spelled the difference between victory and defeat. Since the mercenary stands in the historian's mind for money, disloyalty, heresy, and anti-social behavior—characteristics antithetical to the tidy package of feudalism—he has become the skeleton in the family closet and is mentioned usually with contempt by his and our own contemporaries.

The hired soldier does not fit into the preconception of what feudalism should be, and on that account is ignored. The inquirer after his status is politely referred to the "official muster-roll" which, of course, takes no notice of his existence. But even though the hired warrior does produce a discordant note in medieval society, he was a factor in that society, and to the degree that his presence was of military import must we alter our conception of feudalism. The greater the degree of reliance upon mercenaries the lesser the importance of feudal knights, and the lesser the importance of feudal knights the lesser the effectiveness of feudalism, at least in its military aspects.

The implications of the importance of hired soldiery extend into areas other than those of feudalism and knight-service. If the English rulers did indeed employ mercenaries on the grand scale suggested by the records they must have enjoyed a great amount of latitude in devising and selecting the military institutions which they employed against their enemies. They were apparently not constrained by any preconceived plan of feudal knight-service but could improvise as the occasion demanded. This fluidity goes far to explain the success of the Norman and Angevin kings of England in overcoming feudal inertia and gathering back into their hands the sovereignty which had been dissipated centuries before.

Medieval English military history also has some rightful claims to the conclusions reached concerning mercenaries. The implications here are chiefly in the areas of recruitment, tactics and strategy. The fact that mercenaries occupied critical positions in medieval armies directly challenges the time-honored—as well as time-worn —statement that "between the last struggles of the infantry of the Anglo-Dane and the rise of the pikemen and bowmen of the fourteenth century lies the period of the supremacy of the mail-clad feudal horseman." [3] The cavalry portion of this theory, though not the feudal implication, has been challenged recently by showing that in the course of many medieval conflicts the knights dismounted and fought on foot. They remained feudal knights nonetheless. The discovery that mercenaries figured prominently in these battles goes one step further by casting doubt on the feudal portion of the statement. For mercenaries were the antithesis of feudal warriors. And in all probability they were not mounted soldiers. Although there is little direct evidence to support the pedary nature of mercenaries in the twelfth century, the honorable niche reserved by society for the mounted warrior together with the expense involved in owning and equipping a warhorse, suggests as much.

The widespread use of mercenaries by the English kings also forces us to take a second look at the traditional interpretation placed on medieval tactics and strategy. Methods of warfare differ with the type of fighters employed. But even the quickest glance at medieval warfare shows that sieges were the most common type of engagement.[4] At a siege one professional mercenary foot soldier was worth a dozen cavalrymen, not only because of his training and adaptability but also due to his potentially longer term of service. The feudal knight was trained from youth to perform in open battle where individual courage counted for the most. This is brought home most pointedly when we observe the type of "reserve training" developed in the later Middle Ages to keep the knight proficient. This was the tournament which was designed to highlight the virtue of individual courage in open battle. But this very quality which stood the knight in such good stead in that type of warfare was useless and often harmful in siege warfare. It would be a mistake to endow medieval military leaders with the sophisticated resource management analysis techniques of modern computerized armies. But surely after several decades of siege warfare it must have occurred to even the most unenlightened that a feudal cavalry was inefficient for the conduct of a siege, and that hired foot soldiers were far better suited for the task.

Another institutional area illuminated by this discussion of mercenaries is that of English financial administration. The use of mercenaries is related to this field through the need by English monarchs of sources of revenue and an organized system of collection and disbursement of money to hired soldiers. Richard fitz Nigel, chief financial agent of Henry Plantagenet, was well aware of the connection between mercenaries and financial organization when he wrote his account of the Exchequer in the twelfth century.

After equating the king's power with the amount of money he possesses, Richard refers to mercenaries as the main area of cash expenditure in the kingdom. The twelfth-century English financial documents support this statement with countless entries of money spent for the service and equipment of mercenaries. Although perhaps not the sole reason behind the organization of the Exchequer in the early twelfth century, the need to pay soldiers contributed to the origin of this English institution.

The widespread use of mercenaries by King Stephen (1135–54) helps to fill in a hitherto obscure period in the development of the Exchequer. We possess one Pipe Roll (the annual audit of royal revenues) from the reign of Henry I (1130) and one from each year of Henry II's reign after 1155. Nothing, however, remains from the intervening period of Stephen. The existence of civil war during Stephen's years has led some to conclude that the organization of finances, begun so well by Stephen's predecessor and improved by his successor, broke down completely under Stephen. This is not the only explanation possible for the lack of records. Stephen's heavy reliance on mercenaries suggests that the financial arrangements set up by the first Henry continued to function and allowed Stephen to pay his mercenaries. The absence of records can be explained by attrition suffered in the civil war.

In our own time the intimate relation between war and finance in Anglo-Norman England has formed the subject of an important study, the conclusions of which are pertinent:

> The incidents of tenure by knight-service have left deep and enduring traces upon the records of English history, for those incidents were of permanent importance to the holders of land and to the crown. The shifting expedients of war finance . . . have left but few and faint traces in the records for the Anglo-Norman period, partly because they were shifting expedients and there was therefore less need to preserve any written record of them. . . . It does not therefore follow that these expedients were insignificant at the time or that we must set the political and social history of this period in a rigid framework of feudalism. We do not know how far those who owed knight-service performed it in person.[5]

Thus in the area of English financial institutions a study of mercenaries casts some light on the fluidity of the period and on the ability of English rulers to experiment with new forms. Since the need for a hired soldiery was a factor in the development of the Exchequer it seems fair to conclude that this financial institution was devised to fulfill an immediate need rather than to satisfy a past tradition. More directly traceable to the need for mercenaries was the development of the institution of scutage, or commutation of military service, a forerunner of later systems of taxation. The implications of the rise of this financial institution to the field of feudalism are important. To trace the origin of scutage to the practice of hiring mercenaries is tantamount to tracing the demise of English feudalism to the same source. One of the conditions which had accompanied the rise of feudalism earlier was a scarcity of money. As a result land became the index of wealth. As the volume of money in circulation increased land began to lose its role as a medium of exchange, and those services which were formerly derived from the land came gradually to be performed for cash. Governments began to hire functionaries, entrepreneurs to employ laborers, and kings to hire mercenaries. The institution of scutage was part of this development. It has always been recognized that this process was well along by the fourteenth century and recent studies have pushed it back into the thirteenth. The discovery that mercenaries were used on a substantial scale in the twelfth century extends back even further in time the period when wage service supplanted tenure service. The earliest provable use of scutage dates from the time of William Rufus (1087–1100), although there are indications that the Conqueror himself was familiar with the institution. As with the Exchequer, this is another indication of twelfth-century monarchs experimenting with an institution created by them to satisfy an immediate need.

The three areas of feudal, military and financial institutions merge, therefore, to form the backdrop for the story of the importance of mercenaries in the twelfth century. Before proceeding to that story, however, it is necessary to examine the variety of soldiers who received wages in that century, and the type of evidence that exists to prove the existence and value of mercenaries.

CHAPTER II

Who Were the Mercenaries

THE nebulous nature of medieval records often makes impossible an exact identification of mercenaries. For this reason it is desirable to start the search for mercenaries with a description of what is being sought. A mercenary was a soldier who fought primarily for money rather than for land. Since there were no nations in the twelfth century it is rhetorical to ask whether or not he was a foreigner. He could be English or non-English without distinction. He was probably a foot soldier rather than a mounted warrior. However, the attempt to translate this definition into actual twelfth-century people presents problems since the middle ground between pure mercenary and pure feudal knight was large and undefined. Many, if not all, fighters who followed their lord into battle out of a sense of feudal obligation were also paid. For example, there was a regular wage scale for knights and sergeants in the twelfth and subsequent centuries. On the other hand some mercenaries, although motivated primarily by money, also received land from their employers. Such was the case with William of Ypres, King Stephen's mercenary captain, who received in addition to his wages, large manors in the county of Kent. In light of this ambiguity it becomes necessary at the outset to isolate those types of fighters among whom the cash incentive was uppermost, albeit mixed to some degree with feudal motives.

The first and most obvious group was made up of those who were totally outside feudal arrangements. They are recognizable in contemporary records by their titles which refer either to the primacy of the pecuniary motive (*solidarii, stipendiarii*), to their geographical origin (Brabantines, Aragonese, Basques, Flemings, etc.), to the fact that they were adventurers, accustomed to walking the roads (*ruta, routiers*), or simply to their origin in the lower class (*coterelli*). In all these cases it is clear that these men were adventurers who had severed their social ties and whose military prowess was for sale. The reasons for their instability were as varied as the social history of the period itself. One unfailing source of mercenaries was that large group of younger sons of nobles who, having been disinherited by their fathers, were either uninterested in or incapable of pursuing a career in the Church, and consequently took up the art of war. Political failure at times added to the supply of mercenaries. One of the most famous medieval mercenaries, William of Ypres, turned to professional soldiering largely for this reason. As the grandson of Robert the Frisian, he was the best qualified candidate to succeed to the countship of Flanders in 1119 and again in 1127. Apparently his illegitimacy intervened on both occasions to keep him from the throne. When the English King Henry I died in 1135 the Flemish Count Thierry, against whom William had been unsuccessful, supported the claims of Henry's daughter Matilda to the English throne. William of Ypres thereupon sold his military services to Matilda's rival, Stephen, partly out of preference for the active life of a warrior and partly as an expression of his opposition to the Flemish ruler.

Natural disasters as well as political ones contributed to the social instability of the period by dislocating many men from their homelands—men who turned to fighting for a fee. In 1110 a great flood inundated the coastal area of Flanders and forced an evacuation of that already overpopulated region. Many of these Flemings moved to England where they were granted asylum first in Northumberland and later in Pembrokeshire. This colony became a fertile source of paid soldiery during the reigns of Henry I and his successors. The pressure of overpopulation in other areas of northwest Europe created manpower pools for hired soldiers. Another favorite source of mercenaries for Henry I during the early years of his reign was the region surrounding his continental castles of Domfront and Mont St. Michel. One chronicler describes these Breton mercenaries as "a race of people, poor at home, and seeking abroad to support a toilsome life by foreign service."

Mercenaries of this type are easily identifiable in the sources. Yet the hired soldier is seldom treated in contemporary records as an individual. Although we are occasionally treated to the name of a mercenary leader, such as William of Ypres, Geoffrey Boterel, Alan of Richmond or William of Dover, nothing is to be learned of individual traits or idiosyncrasies. Medieval literature speaks of mercenaries only in corporate terms, lumping them into a homogeneous block, each member of which is cut from the same pattern. There is simply no historical basis for an accurate description of those items of the individual's life and work which we would desperately like to know. Nevertheless, it is possible to isolate some class characteristics of mercenaries which form recurring themes among the chroniclers. Some of these are good, others bad. The foremost undesirable trait was their greed, cruelty and harsh treatment of the Church personnel and property. During the reign of King Stephen an eyewitness wrote the following description:

> To crown all these evils there was the fact that a savage crowd of barbarians, who had swarmed to England in a body to serve as mercenaries, were affected neither by bowels of compassion nor by feelings of human pity over sufferings so many and so great, but everywhere in the castles they conspired with one mind to commit crime and outrage, were unceasingly occupied in pillaging the goods of the poor, devoted all the zeal of their evil hearts to encouraging hostility on both sides and murdering men in every quarter.[1]

Undoubtedly the fact that historians of this time were clerics explains somewhat their obsession with these items. Furthermore, the chroniclers were not above taking sides, and their descriptions often reflected their own political hues. The overall impression remains, nonetheless, that mercenaries were looked down upon by the Church and society in general and were tolerated only because of their military and political value.

But even to grant the basic truth of these assertions of greed and cruelty is not to rule out their usefulness in military action. And their value here is undeniable. Actually, statements attesting to their faithfulness and sense of professionalism overshadow those describing their social disabilities. William Rufus, for example, is reported to have rewarded the faithfulness of his mercenaries with a multitude of gifts. On his deathbed Henry I ordered £6000 to be distributed to his servants and hired troops as gifts. "As for Stephen, there were few upon whom he could implicitly rely besides his Flemish mercenaries under William of Ypres." [2] An interesting incident during the revolt against Henry I in 1102 illustrates the professional pride that existed among hired forces. A contingent of stipendiary troops fought alongside the regular garrison which was defending the castle of Bridgnorth for Robert of Bellême against Henry. When the feudal and urban forces capitulated the mercenaries wished to continue the defense lest the disaster be considered a slur on the character of mercenaries. This incident indicates that at the beginning of the twelfth century a feeling of solidarity existed among mercenaries.

Kings were not the only military leaders to use mercenaries in the twelfth century. Hired soldiers were frequently found in the employ of barons and tenants-in-chief. This is significant since the chroniclers often remark the presence at medieval battles of the most prominent tenants-in-chief but rarely refer to their followers except as "their men." Since the barons were in the habit of employing paid soldiers there is no more reason to believe that "their men" were feudal knights than that they were mercenaries. Yet it seems to be taken for granted that the presence of a handful of barons at a military engagement meant the presence of the "feudal array." A few examples of baronial use of mercenaries should dispel this misinterpretation. In 1070 Abbot Turold of Peterborough employed 160 mercenaries to defend his monastery against Hereward. Robert of Bellême, Earl of Shrewsbury, hired scores of soldiers to assist him in his rebellion against Henry I in 1102. In Stephen's time we find mercenaries in the employ of most of the important lords of the kingdom, including Reginald of Cornwall, Ranulph of Chester, and Bishop Nigel of Ely (1140), the King's own brother, Henry of Winchester (1141 and 1148), Henry of Anjou during his English campaigns of 1147 and 1153, and Hugh of Puiset (1148). The same was true during Henry II's reign. Stipendiary troops were used by Robert, Earl of Leicester, in 1173 and Hugh, Earl of Norfolk, in 1174. These are but a few samples, but enough to show that the

English tenants-in-chief during the twelfth century were accustomed to hiring mercenaries. We do not know how often they did so to fulfill their military obligation to the king. There is no reason to doubt that this became a standard practice before the century was over.

Less easy to discern than these mercenaries that were identified as such in the records were those warriors who fought primarily for pay but whose monetary motives were mixed to varying degrees or from time to time with feudal ones. These fighters, all of whom are to be considered mercenaries, are found throughout the pages of the records performing in one of three different capacities. First there were the household retainers who received pay rather than land for their services, even though such service was inspired partly by feudal obligation. Secondly, there were the fief-rentiers—fighters whose services had been contracted for by rich and powerful rulers. Finally, there must be included in the ranks of mercenaries those feudal knights who continued to campaign with the king after their period of feudal service had expired. These knights were paid for the service they performed "above and beyond the call of duty," and were mercenaries at least part of the time. In each of these three cases the motives of the warriors were partly feudal and partly non-feudal. In each, however, it was the non-feudal, monetary element which predominated.

The institution of the household retainer developed in the Anglo-Norman period immediately after the Conquest as the result of the insufficiency of land for William I to reward all his followers. Many fighters attached themselves to royal, and even baronial, households for pay. This was not an entirely new arrangement in England, since these retainers in many ways resembled the Anglo-Saxon housecarles and thegns who had formed the *comitatus* of the pre-Conquest English kings. They "constituted a large and significant class throughout the Anglo-Norman age and played an important part in the so-called feudal host." Retainers were more common in the early Anglo-Norman period than later on, since as land became available they tended to slip into the feudal ranks. Nevertheless, there were still quite a few such mercenaries in existence a century after Hastings, as is clear from the *Cartae Baronum* of 1166. Unfortunately the preoccupation of the official records of the Anglo-

Norman period with enfeoffment has resulted in almost total silence on the subject of household soldiers. Occasionally we get glimpses of them in the chronicles, as in the case of John fitz Gilbert, the royal marshal under Stephen, who paid and kept three-hundred soldiers in his household, or the retainers who helped Bishop Wulfstan of Worcester repel a Welsh invasion during the reign of William Rufus. But for the most part the records refer to these retainers with titles so general as to be equally applicable to enfeoffed knights, members of the militia, or mercenaries. Wherever their presence can be reasonably inferred, however, they must be treated as mercenaries since they represented a predominantly non-feudal element, they occupied an important place in royal and baronial armies of the early twelfth century, and they were paid.

For the same reasons fighters supplied by the money fief (fief-rentiers) must be considered mercenaries. A money fief was an arrangement whereby one ruler promised to come to the aid of another with a stipulated number of warriors in return for an annual stipend. As with the household retainers, an element of feudal obligation surrounded the money fief, but this element was more in the nature of a lingering tradition than of a dynamic force. It was overshadowed by the money involved. Since the money fief was essentially military and monetary, the soldiers produced by this bargain were mercenaries. Some writers have suggested that the money fief was essentially a diplomatic rather than a military weapon, by which rulers extended their feudal relationships beyond their own domains. However an examination of all money fiefs granted over a four-hundred-year period (starting in 1101) suggests a direct proportion between the number of fiefs contracted and the amount of military activity in progress. This indicates that this institution served a military, not a diplomatic, purpose, and opens the way for the acceptance of the fighters produced by it as mercenaries. That the exchange of money was an integral part of the arrangement is indicated by the direct correlation between the amount of money expended on the one hand, and the number of fighters agreed upon on the other. The most famous money fief in English history was the one of 1101 by which Henry I of England promised to pay Count Robert II of Flanders an annual stipend of £500 in return for the services of one thousand soldiers for the defense of England and Normandy and five hundred warriors to protect Maine. When this agreement was renewed seven years later the amount of money was reduced almost by half (to four hundred marks), and so was the number of soldiers promised (to five hundred). The implication that less money bought less soldiers indicates the primacy of cash and the secondary importance of the feudal element in these transactions. The money fief was a new institution in the early twelfth century, and its principal history begins some two centuries later. Yet, even as early as the twelfth century the description of this institution as having one foot in feudalism and one in the money economy should be modified so as to place one toe in the old and nine in the new.

The third type of fighter who was partly feudal and partly mercenary was the feudal knight who continued to fight after the expiration of his obligatory period of service and who was paid for this extended duty. The records are not clear concerning the exact amount of annual military service that was expected from the enfeoffed knight. In pre-Conquest England the annual tour of duty was sixty days. In Normandy during the same period a charter of the Conqueror relating to the Abbey of Mont St. Michel stipulates that the first forty days of service were to be performed at the vassal's expense, but that the cost of any further service must be charged to the lord. In the thirteenth century English knights were expected to devote forty days, or an equivalent, each year to military service. A recent evaluation of this evidence shows that in the twelfth century the old English custom of sixty days continued in force until the time of Stephen when the barons were strong enough to force a reduction to the forty days which was customary in Normandy.[3] That knights were paid for this extra service in the twelfth century seems fairly certain although here again no direct statement to this effect has been uncovered. It has already been mentioned that such was the Norman custom. Instances of such payments are common in England in the following century. In 1212 King John ordered that certain knights should be paid from the royal treasury "from the time when the period shall have elapsed during which they are bound to serve at their own cost." The Norman and later English customs add up to a reasonable certainty that this was also the twelfth-century practice of English kings.

Modern authors and commentators of the period assume such an arrangement as a matter of course.

A survey of military campaigns and sieges shows that many of the campaigns between 1066 and 1189—especially on the Continent —lasted longer than the accepted term of service, be it forty or sixty days.[4] Therefore conversion of knights to mercenary status was a common occurrence. Furthermore, it became an increasingly common phenomenon as the twelfth century progressed. The number of military engagements swelled dramatically during the reign of Henry II who was involved with regularity in continental campaigns. It was precisely at the time of increased military activity that the annual term of service decreased from sixty to forty days. Thus it would seem that more and more knights were paid more and more money to remain on for longer and longer periods of military service as the century wore on.

Despite the theoretical importance of these three semi-mercenary groups, it is impossible to discover how widely they were used. Although household retainers were numerous immediately after the Conquest, their numbers dwindled as they gradually became enfeoffed. The money fief was just getting started in the twelfth century and didn't reach its height until the fourteenth century. The number of knights remaining to fight after their period of obligation had expired could not have been too large since the number of knights on campaign in fulfillment of this feudal requirement was itself very small. This last point is crucial to the whole question of the use of mercenaries. Not only is it true that "we do not know how far those who owed knight-service performed it in person," but there are increasing signs that knight-service was, or at least quickly became, a fiscal arrangement used to produce money, not warriors.

The strictly military records and accounts, however, tell only part of the story. There were several vital and practical obstacles to the existence of an effective system of knight-service in medieval England—objections which point toward the ubiquity of mercenaries and reinforce the already strong impression derived directly from the military accounts. One argument against its effectiveness is the obvious incongruity of a system which expected military service from babies, women, monks, the crippled, the senile and even cowards. As fiefs became hereditary there were many instances when land, and military service, devolved upon such as these. Neither health, maturity, nor military expertise were prerequisites for the inheritance of land. The simplest and most equitable solution was the system of commutation whereby the obligation of military service was satisfied through a money payment. The money could then be used to hire mercenaries. The same solution was used to get around another practical difficulty. As subinfeudation progressed down the scale, the amount of service expected grew smaller and smaller until we read of instances where a piece of land was enfeoffed for the minute portion of a knight's fee. This process had started early in the twelfth century and we have several examples from the reign of Henry I where land was granted for the service of as little as one-twentieth of a knight's fee. By 1166 a significant proportion of all knights' fees listed in the survey of that year were for the service of one-half, or less, of a knight.[5]

It is conceivable, but impractical, that landowners owing such fractions banded together so that each sent, on a rotating basis, one knight to represent the group. It is much more likely that such service was converted into a cash payment, used by the lord to hire mercenaries.

The machinery for such commutation existed by the time of Henry I in the form of scutage. Although there is some circumstantial evidence to support the existence of scutage before 1100, the first pieces of direct evidence start arriving in that year. Specific mention is made of commutation in the years 1100, 1101, 1107, 1119, ca. 1120, 1127, and 1130. Only this last instance, that of 1130, is derived from an official source, the Pipe Roll of that year. Since this is the sole surviving Pipe Roll of Henry's reign, however, the mention of scutage in it is highly significant. Commutation was not restricted to the holders of fractional knights' fees, but was employed as well by those who owed substantial numbers of fighters. The privilege—if indeed that is what it was—belonged during the early part of the century to ecclesiastical fief holders only. Later it was extended to all. The advantages provided by this alternate plan to knight-service must surely have been apparent to those embarrassed to find that their land had fallen into the hands of the militarily unfit, or had been hopelessly split into infinitesimal fractions. By Henry II's time scutage was a fully recognized substitute for knight-service and the rate of money collected in lieu of service was directly proportional to the cost of hiring a mercenary substitute.

There is another serious obstacle to the theory that knight-service effectively produced an army in medieval England and this is the persistence of disloyalty in Anglo-Norman times. Students of feudalism have shown quite rightly that loyalty was the mortar which cemented the entire feudal edifice. Among the ancestral German tribes of the first century A.D., who were responsible for many of the elements of later feudalism, disloyalty and the "abandonment of the shield" were looked upon as the basest of crimes. Hanging, the most serious punishment, was reserved for traitors and deserters. An incisive picture of the importance of loyalty and the disgrace attendant upon treason is painted by the words of Wiglaf scornfully addressing those companions who deserted Beowulf in the face of the fiery dragon:

> Now, all sharing of treasure, all gifts of swords, all hope, all rights of home, shall cease from your kin. Every man of your house shall roam, bereft of tribal rights, as soon as the princes in far countries hear of your flight, your inglorious deed. Death is better for every man than a life of shame! [6]

How else could it be in a society whose bonds were personal and whose warriors served the personality of their leaders rather than the cold dictates of bloodless institutions. Their descendants in the feudal period were expected to act no less from a sense of personal loyalty. The very contract whereby a vassal promised military—or other—service to his lord stressed loyalty and faithfulness on the part of both parties. "I swear upon these four Gospels of God that I will always be a faithful vassal to thee and to thy successors" is a recurring statement in the feudal act of homage. The classic statement by Fulbert of Chartres early in the eleventh century concerning the reciprocal duties of lord and vassal discusses six items which constituted the feudal bond. All six are variations on the theme of loyalty. Yet the political history of England from William's conquest in 1066 to the death of his second son Henry I, in 1135, is one in which loyalty is conspicuous by its absence. Deprived of many of their chief feudal assistants, the Anglo-Norman rulers were forced to hire soldiers in their bid to remain on the English throne. Equally disruptive of a neat and orderly feudal arrangement was divided loyalty. The fact that faithfulness attained such prominence in feudal literature and became the keystone of the system is an indication that it was the one element hardest to come by and the one that had to be stressed most often to keep the machinery intact. It was also the most sensitive. The slightest shift in balance would knock the entire system askew. As subinfeudation increased, many a vassal came to find himself beholden to several lords, each with equally weighty claims to his service. In theory feudalism assumed a unity of command. In practice it could not survive without it. Developments during the reign of Stephen (1135–54) bear this out. Not until the War of the Roses in the fifteenth century was England again to witness such a period of divided loyalties as during the contest between Stephen and Matilda. The result was an unabashed suspension of whatever feudal rules still existed as both sides employed mercenaries on a large scale. As the barons were changing sides with alarming regularity, the only stable factor was the hired soldiery whose military performance accounted for whatever decisive military engagements took place. This period has often been pictured as disruptive of financial, political, administrative and religious institutions. But even more important is its role in dealing the death blow to knight-service. For whereas Stephen's reign brought only a temporary setback to these other institutions, which subsequently returned with renewed strength, English military institutions were never the same afterwards. This period of divided loyalties was a watershed in the history of military feudalism. It turned military organization in a new direction. Once the feudal barons had had a taste of the ease with which they could defy the king, and the effectiveness and simplicity of hiring soldiers, they never returned to the earlier arrangements.

Stephen's successor, Henry II, relied on mercenaries for different reasons. As a strong king—in many ways the strongest in medieval England—he suffered seriously neither from disloyalty nor from disunity. His problem was disinterest. So well did he restore unity to the country that the habits of peace supplanted those of war. The martial spirit gradually decayed in Henry's England. The barons, formerly devoted to military interests, turned more and more to peaceful pursuits. Their service slowly metamorphosed to the large-scale administrative, financial and judicial tasks required in such a highly organized state. Not that Henry did not have wars. He had plenty of them, especially on the Continent. But the barons exhibited a striking lack of interest in following the King to war. Consequently Henry relied on mercenaries who, for a fee, were always available and would serve as long as the King had need of them. Thanks to Henry's efficient organization of England's finances, he was in an economically sound position to hire men to carry out the multifarious activities connected with war. Soldiers, engineers, ship captains, and castle guardians appear regularly on his payroll. He turned as many feudal arrangements as he could into money-making institutions. By making royal justice available to virtually all Englishmen Henry was motivated by more than a desire for political and legal centralization. Writs of admission to the royal court cost money. He investigated the sheriffs to make sure that he was getting all the money that he could expect from the counties. He stretched the feudal aid customarily collected upon marriage of the kings' daughters to such lengths that the complaints against his exactions found their way into the chronicles of the period. In short, he charged all that the traffic would bear. And the money collected by these methods was spent largely for fighting men to serve in the place of feudal knights who had settled down and lost the ways of war. In the face of this it is difficult to interpret his survey of knights' fees in 1166 in any other light than as another in a series of attempts to convert a sickly feudal tradition into a healthy source of income.

"The Normans have always been restless and have persistently fomented rebellion."
———Orderic Vitalis

CHAPTER III

William I And His Sons

IF loyalty was the mortar of feudalism the feudal edifice was weak indeed in England during the reigns of the Anglo-Norman kings (1066–1135). The story of Norman disloyalty did not begin with William's invasion but can be traced back to those continental days before William traded the title of "Bastard" for the much more impressive one of "Conqueror." On the day when Harold of England both lived and died William had behind him thirty-one years of experience ruling and controlling the Norman baronage. During this period he came to learn at first hand that racial unity and loyalty were not Norman traits. Although the Normans could on occasion exhibit a sense of cohesion when threatened from outside their province—such as in 1048 by Geoffrey Martel of Anjou, and in 1054 and 1058 by the French king, Henry I—internecine struggle was more characteristic of these descendants of Rolf.

William's acquaintance with Norman infidelity began at an early age. The dozen years of his ducal minority has aptly been described as one of the darkest periods in Norman history.[1] What made it so were the machinations of his countrymen and supposedly faithful followers who tried to replace him. That he was able to survive his minority at all was due to the intervention on his behalf of his overlord, King Henry I of France, who feared to see one of his fiefs lapse into a state of anarchy. From the day he assumed personal rule of Normandy in 1047, until he became master of England, William waged a ceaseless war for survival against the personal ambitions of his countrymen.

Although domestic struggle was continuous throughout the

period, it reached the point of revolt on four occasions. The first occurred in the very year of William's majority when his Burgundian cousin, Guy, considering his own legitimate birth a better credential than William's for the dukedom of Normandy, attempted to seize the duke and the duchy. As before, Henry I of France supported his vassal and took the lead in defeating the rebels at Val-es-Dunes. So threatening was internal disloyalty that outside aid was needed. A similar plot in the following year by William, Count of Mortain, never reached the point of action because the Duke, hearing of it, deprived him of his county. About the same time William Busac of Eu saw his plans to overthrow the Duke frustrated when he was exiled and his land confiscated. In 1052 a major rebellion took place, led by William's uncle, William of Arques, who renounced his vassalage and gained strong support from the other Norman barons. Of significance was the involvement on the side of the rebels of the Archbishop of Rouen, the head of the Norman church. The impression gained from these accounts of the Norman baronage is one that should dispel any image of a homogeneous, well-knit race of men prepared to impose unity on the kingdom across the Channel.

The descriptions of these pre-Conquest military ventures in Normandy are too scanty to permit a firm judgment about the use of mercenaries by Duke William. The chroniclers become no more specific than to mention the presence of "foot-soldiers," or of the calling out of the "neighborhood peasants." And even though examples of the use of paid troops had been provided much earlier by William's distant relatives in England, it would be stretching the evidence to state categorically that he imitated this policy in these early campaigns. All that can be said with any degree of certainty is that the Norman duke was in a better financial position to hire soldiers than were either his barons or his neighbors. Normandy's fiscal organization in the eleventh century was much more sophisticated and productive of hard cash than was that of any of the duchy's neighbors. Ducal power was relatively strong and it had a sound economic basis in the commercial activity of the towns bordering the Channel. These cities gave the ruler of the duchy a decided advantage over his adversaries. In addition, there is every indication that Normandy got off to an early start in the development of its financial institutions. Under William's grand-father, Duke Richard II (996–1026), a treasury existed and the distinction between ordinary and extraordinary income was rec-ognized. During William's reign the collection of fixed revenues became systematized. Vicomtes had the job of collecting ducal resources from the territories. An extant list of these revenues sug-gests that they were extensive and well organized, and included feudal as well as non-feudal items. In general, the eleventh-century Norman dukes were niggardly with their sources of revenue and seldom allowed them to fall into the hands of their subordinates.

This was in sharp contrast to the institutional situation in neighboring areas. While William was struggling valiantly and with a goodly measure of success to concentrate revenues in his own hands, Anjou to the south was headed in the opposite direction. There the eleventh century was a period of eclipse for the Count's power. In Brittany the ducal position was to remain weak for another century and only began to recoup its losses with Geoffrey in 1181. Even the Ile de France, the home of William's lord, Henry I, was the scene of a struggle by the descendants of Hugh Capet to maintain whatever political and financial assets had been handed down to them. They succeeded in preserving the status quo only through a liberal policy of granting revenue-laden franchises to their vassals. Only in Normandy, therefore, was there a discernible movement toward centralization of finances and consequently only that duchy was in a financial position favorable to the employment of mercenaries. Whether or not ancestral tradition, Norman in-fidelity, and a brimming treasury coalesced to provide William with stipendiary troops cannot be learned from the sources. It would seem strange if such were not the case, however, especially in light of his later readiness to use mercenaries.

The Norman propensity toward rugged individualism and disagreement with their lord did not cease with the relative peace which the duchy enjoyed between 1060 and 1066. Even the stimulus of the proposal to invade England was insufficient to inject any large degree of loyalty into the Norman baronage. Apparently William was hard put to persuade most of his barons of the wisdom of this venture. Many Norman war councils must have preceded the departure of the Norman invasion force in September, 1066, but we have details of only two. The first was held at Lillebonne and was called to discuss preparations for the invasion of England. William's inner council was present, composed of his two half-brothers, Odo of Bayeux and Robert, Count of Mortain, as well as Roger of Montgomery, Walter Giffard, William fitz Osbern, Robert, Count of Eu, and Roger of Beaumont. This meeting ended with the barons in full agreement and pledging support for the expedition. However, at a subsequent assembly of the entire baronage, probably at Caen, there were complaints and disloyal mutterings against the plan. An anonymous list of the donations of men and ships pledged by the barons contains the names of but fourteen lords.[2] Seven of these were the men present at the first meeting who were responsible for the original decision. If this list is anywhere near complete it indicates that William and his council were able to convince only seven additional Norman leaders to support the Duke's plans. This gives statistical support to the statement of Henry of Huntingdon that very few of the lords were disposed to follow the Duke.[3]

But even had the Conqueror enjoyed the undivided support of the entire Norman force this would have fallen short of the requirements for such an operation. The maximum number of Normans he could have squeezed from the duchy at their own expense was about two thousand. To send such a force across the Channel William would have had to strip Normandy and leave it defenseless in the face of ravenous neighbors. Therefore it is probable that the number of his vassals in the Conqueror's army was far less than that figure. The remaining positions were filled with mercenaries of one stripe or another. William's call for support was answered by adventurers from the neighboring lands of Flanders, Brittany, Poitou, Burgundy, Maine, and the Ile de France, and even from the more distant regions of southern France and Italy.

Some of these mercenaries were paid outright while others were willing to wait for their reward in the form of land across the water. The latter was true of many of the Flemings who joined the expedition. The Domesday survey of 1086 lists at least fifteen Flemish tenants-in-chief and hundreds of lesser Flemish lords in the southern and eastern counties of England. Not all of William's mercenaries were so patient, however, and many, presumably of the less noble variety, were paid and supported from the outset. Especially during the trying month of September, as the assembled forces awaited a wind favorable to the fleet, William was generous to his hired soldiers, supplying them with food and money. Once the island was secured those mercenaries who did not receive land for their participation were paid handsomely before returning to the Continent.

The Battle of Hastings has been analyzed from almost every aspect, and the flood of literature which has accompanied the recent celebration of the nonocentenary of the event leaves little room for addition to the general description of this famous battle. If Orderic is to be believed, the mercenaries did not comport themselves particularly well. First the Bretons and then the Flemings fled the scene of battle. Much credit for the victory is given on William's side to the Norman cavalry, and on Harold's to that king's fatigue or poor strategy in deciding upon the defensive. Be that as it may, it was the continental army that emerged the victor, and it was an army composed essentially of mercenaries.

It is at this point that historians speak of the introduction into England of what amounts to virtually a new social arrangement whose cohesive force lay in the personal agreement between lord and vassal based ultimately upon mutual loyalty. That this latter virtue was not a trait particularly strong among Normans has already been noted. Nor was it suddenly acquired along with the new lands and responsibilities. The evidence points to the fact that the earlier propensity toward restlessness and revolt was magnified in the new land, rendering impossible the successful operation of any system based upon mutual cooperation. The period of Norman rule in England, which terminated with Stephen's accession in 1135, saw little change in the Normans' centrifugal tendencies. William I, having experienced this temperament at work both before and during the move to England, restrained it with a strong hand. His two sons, however, embodied this rebellious nature in themselves and were unable to overcome it in others to the degree required for the successful implementation of a "feudal system."

One way to measure the degree of disloyalty in England during the period 1066–1135—and in the process suggest the unreliability of the system of knight-service—is to follow the fortunes of the

Conqueror's leading supporters at Hastings after their arrival in England. The Domesday survey of 1086, in which William audited his English land, serves as a useful instrument for this purpose. Since wealth was measured in land in the eleventh century, it is not difficult to discover who were the important people in England. The preparation of a list of the holdings for the approximately 120 lords who shared in the settlement would take us too far afield. However, a representative sampling of the top ten landholders is enlightening.[4] The lands of two of the ten, William fitz Osbern and Ralph the Staller, were forfeited through disloyalty and returned to the Conqueror even before the survey was taken. This in itself is strong proof of the continuation of discontent. Of the remaining eight landholders, five rebelled at least once before the century was over —either in person or through their sons. William of Warrenne, of the remaining three, raised the banner of revolt in 1101. By 1135 only two had kept their record clean, but the descendant of one of these, Geoffrey of Mandeville, was soon to become a household word for infidelity and faithlessness. Were the list extended to include the lower echelon of Norman landholders it would no doubt reveal an equally high incidence of disloyalty and disunity.

William's honeymoon in England with the Normans lasted about nine years. The newness of it all, coupled with the common objective of pacifying the Anglo-Saxon malcontents, tended to overshadow Norman individualism. Once the common threat subsided, however, the barons wasted no time in returning to their former state of restlessness. William faced the first internal challenge to his rule in 1075. This came from Roger, Earl of Hereford, the son of William fitz Osbern, who had been the Conqueror's chief confidant in Normandy and during the invasion of 1066. At the distribution of spoils after Hastings, William fitz Osbern had received the lion's share which made him the leading landholder among William's followers. Upon his death in Flanders in 1071, his lands passed to his son Roger who four years later saw fit to challenge William's position. Significantly, Roger was joined by Ralph of Gael, the son of another of William's leading supporters, Ralph the Staller. The pretext for the revolt was the King's refusal to allow Ralph to marry Roger's sister. But behind it was Roger's irritation at William's attempt, through his sheriff, to hold pleas in Roger's land.

The Conqueror was in Normandy at the time and relied upon his justiciars, William of Warrenne and Richard of Bienfaite to handle the situation. This does not indicate that he was unconcerned or that he considered the revolt of minor consequence. The importance of the rebellion can be gauged from a series of letters that passed between Lanfranc, Archbishop of Canterbury, and the rebels. In the first letter, written to Roger, Lanfranc reminded the Earl of his father's loyalty to William and suggested that he imitate it. He also promised to suspend the irritant which had led to the revolt, but to no avail. The second letter was much stronger. In it Roger was exhorted to free himself from the charge of disloyalty. Lanfranc's third and final epistle despaired of the Earl's repentance and excommunicated him.

Military action in this uprising took place almost solely in the land of Ralph, who was Earl of Norfolk and Suffolk. The revolt was put down by a combination of "Norman and English," a phrase which tells us nothing of the actual composition of the royal forces. However, Lanfranc's description of the siege and occupation of Norwich castle, relates that three hundred men-at-arms, including crossbowmen and engineers, were among the occupying forces— obviously not feudal knights, but warriors paid for their specialized services. Since the siege of the castle lasted more than three months the royalists must have relied heavily upon mercenaries. As a result of their rashness, both Roger and Ralph lost their lands. The former was imprisoned for life, the latter fled.

Therefore less than a decade after his seizure of England King William was stung by a resurgence of that Norman faithlessness which had kept him constantly occupied in his homeland. But it was precisely at this time, the early 1070's, that he is supposed, according to Round, to have introduced the military policy of knight-service which depended for its manpower upon the loyalty of the baronage. Had William even contemplated such an arrangement, this revolt of the Earl of Hereford must have given him second thoughts in the matter. The successful use of non-feudal and possibly mercenary elements to quell the rebellion must have impressed upon the Conqueror their potential as a counterpoise to treason.

During William's second and final decade on the English throne he experienced two more significant revolts. And they came closer to home. The first, in 1078, centered around William's own son, Robert Curthose, on the Continent. The slowness with which the Conqueror fulfilled his promise to grant Robert the sovereignty of Maine and Normandy alienated his son who turned to the French king and some Norman lords for support. As in the revolt of three years earlier, the sons of two of William's leading tenants-in-chief were involved. Among the discontented were Robert of Bellême, son of Roger of Montgomery, and William of Breteuil, another son of William fitz Osbern.

Curthose's failure against his father in this attempt was due to the King's use of mercenaries. The campaign was fought entirely on the Continent, where Robert gathered about him, in addition to the Norman barons, confederates from France and Brittany, Maine and Anjou. William relied on hired forces, including those of the Lord of Mortain. The mercenaries of the King were paid with money derived from the land which he had confiscated from Robert's adherents.

William was acutely aware of the tenuousness of Norman loyalty. In the course of an argument with his son prior to this revolt the Conqueror, by way of warning, referred to that faithlessness which he had come to recognize over the years from bitter experience:

> The Normans have always been restless, and have persistently fomented rebellion. Now they have led you to act foolishly, so that they might use you as a shield for their disloyal actions.[5]

Although the warning went unheeded, it is indicative of the depth of William's distrust of his own people and suggests that he would hesitate to depend solely upon them for military aid.

A further dramatic instance of disloyalty came four years later when William imprisoned his half-brother and fellow adventurer at Hastings, Odo Bishop of Bayeux. Odo was the Earl of Kent and the richest of the Conqueror's tenants. During the revolt of Roger and Ralph seven years earlier, Odo had served the absent King faithfully and was one of the chief instruments in quelling the disturbance. The motive and indeed the very nature of Odo's crime in 1082 is not known with certainty. At his trial he was accused by William of trying to steal the riches of the kingdom, of turning the heads of the King's knights from the Conqueror, and of spreading disorder throughout the realm: in short, of political disloyalty while the King was away in Normandy. Odo's activity here was possibly inspired by his aspirations to replace Gregory VII on the papal throne. At any rate he was imprisoned where he remained until William's death five years later.

It is hard to see any change in the pattern of disloyalty before or after the Conquest. Events between 1047 and 1087 display an amazing evenness. When threatened from without, whether from France or Anjou in the earlier period or from the conquered English later on, the Normans were capable of temporary cooperation. But the disappearance of external pressure invariably resulted in internal fragmentation as the lords and even the family of the Conqueror turned against him. To an ever increasing degree William met these threats with mercenaries. So accustomed had he become to relying upon them that in 1085 when he was threatened by yet another invasion, this time from the Danes and Flemings, he imported vast hordes of hired fighting men "from all of Gaul," and quartered them on the lands of his vassals throughout England. How many they were can be deduced from the chroniclers who report that their numbers oppressed the kingdom and that people wondered how the land could feed so many. Although the Danes never carried out the invasion, William's preparations on this occasion justify the conclusion that "in a great emergency the knight-service due to the king from his tenants-in-chief was obviously unequal to the defense of the land." [6]

With the disappearance in 1087 of the Conqueror's relatively strong restraining hand his sons' querulousness moved up from the baronial to the royal level. Where the first William had suffered several revolts which were quickly extinguished, the second experienced major rebellions which resulted in the permanent alienation of many of the important people of the realm. Again, where the Conqueror had found occasional need to supplement his "feudal array" with hired soldiers, Rufus came to depend almost entirely upon mercenaries. Between 1087 and the end of the century the increased incidence of disloyalty resulted in an increased dependence on paid troops. The King's method of raising money to pay the soldiers is reflected in a contemporary complaint:

From the very beginning of his reign, through fear of revolt, he gathered soldiers and denied them nothing, promising them even greater rewards later on; consequently he soon drained his father's treasury and had but moderate resources. . . . He lacked a good head for business: a trader could sell him something for any price, and soldiers could demand any pay they pleased. . . . News of his generosity spread through the west and even reached the east. Military men flocked to him from every province this side of the mountains, and he paid them most handsomely. As a result he ran out of money and turned to rapine.[7]

The revolts which William Rufus feared were not long in coming. Behind them lay the perennial ambitions of his brother, Robert Curthose, to occupy the English throne. The settlement at the Conqueror's death, according to which William Rufus ascended the English throne and Robert received the duchy of Normandy, did not satisfy his ambitions. Early in 1088 Robert's supporters led uprisings throughout England aimed at deposing the Red King. Among the leading barons in revolt were Odo of Bayeux—but recently released from confinement—Robert, Count of Mortain, Roger of Montgomery and his son Robert of Bellême, Geoffrey Bishop of Coutances, and Eustace of Boulogne, all strong supporters of the original Norman invasion. These were joined by other important barons who had recently sworn fidelity to the new king. Although it is probably true that the majority of English lords remained faithful or at best indifferent to William, those in revolt included the most politically important segment of the realm. An eyewitness has characterized them as "men whose vast landed possessions gave them great preponderance in England."[8]

Deprived of the loyalty of the Normans, the King relied upon the clergy and mercenaries to put down the revolt. He assembled the English, both infantry and cavalry, at London where he promised them many rewards for their service. Although rebellion took place in such widely varied areas as Kent, Hereford, Norfolk, Sussex and Somerset, we have extended accounts of military events at but two: Worcester and Rochester. In both cases mercenaries were employed in the King's cause. At Worcester Bishop Wulfstan defeated the rebels with his retainers, while the siege of Rochester was carried

out with paid soldiers. The rebels were defeated and their confiscated land distributed to the mercenaries who were responsible
for the King's victory.

This note of disloyalty which marked the opening of the
second William's reign convinced the King of the need to amplify
his sources of military manpower as a hedge against future baronial
defection. With the support of his justiciar and treasurer, Ranulph
Flambard, Bishop of Durham, William was equal to the task.
Ranulph's fund-raising measures would do credit to the most
imaginative modern government or university alumni group. The
chroniclers described them as "rapine." Burdensome taxes and exactions were levied upon the entire kingdom. No class within the
realm escaped. Bishoprics and abbacies were purposely left vacant
upon the death of their incumbents for long periods of time to
create an additional channel of revenue into the royal treasury. For
example, after Lanfranc's death in 1089, his See of Canterbury was
purposely kept unfilled. It was so profitable to the King that a new
Archbishop was not appointed until four years later, and only then
because the remorseful Rufus saw his end approaching during a
royal illness. Parish priests were often made to pay for the privilege
of receiving their new churches. Nobles swelled the fund through
"gifts" in order to gain their inheritances. In 1098, for instance,
Robert of Bellême "donated" £3000 to the King so that he might
succeed to his brother's earlship of Shrewsbury. Granaries and
merchants' stores were ransacked under orders from the chief
justiciar. A gift to the King was even capable of loosening the halter
around a robber's neck. The ultimate destination of much of this
money was the pay envelope of the mercenary.

In addition to these relatively common fund raising devices
there now appeared a new one—commutation, for a price, of military obligation. This practice, called scutage, is not mentioned
earlier in Anglo-Norman England and the evidence for its existence
even during Rufus' reign is indirect. The familiar manner used to
refer to it in a charter of 1100, however, strongly suggests that it
existed before that date. In 1094 William, threatened once again
with invasion by his brother, summoned a large force of Englishmen—possibly militia—to gather at Hastings and ordered Ranulph
to collect ten shillings from each soldier and dismiss them. It is

clear from the accounts that the money was collected in lieu of military service and was sent to the Continent to purchase military substitutes. Although the name was lacking, the elements of scutage were present and the practice of hiring mercenaries took a step forward towards becoming institutionalized.

The invasion never took place, but in the following year the King faced a major revolt, this time on the part of the northern barons, who planned to murder William and put Stephen d'Aumule on the throne. Prominent among the rebels were the descendants of many key barons who had been disloyal in earlier days. It was spearheaded by Robert of Mowbray, the Earl of Northumberland and heir to the 280 manors of his uncle Geoffrey, Bishop of Coutances, and Hugh of Montgomery, the second son of Roger of Montgomery. Both Geoffrey and Roger had tried without success to topple William seven years earlier. Roger of Lacy, the son of yet another companion of the Conqueror, joined the conspiracy. The King sent his other brother, Henry, to Normandy to handle a simultaneous uprising there while he remained in England to take personal charge of suppressing the rebels. On the Continent the royal forces were composed almost entirely of mercenaries. The campaign in England lasted five months, suggesting that hired soldiers were used to supplement the feudal forces.

In 1096 Curthose departed on the First Crusade. In order to raise money for the pious expedition he mortgaged Normandy to William. With this reunion of Norman holdings rebellion in England became muted. Along with the privileges of Normandy William inherited the responsibilities, not the least of which was that of defending the duchy from avaricious neighbors. He could not, however, depend totally on Norman support and the military forces he employed in his newly acquired land were hired from surrounding areas. In his contest in 1097 with Philip of France over the Vexin, William won over most of the French to his side by his wealth. In the following year French, Burgundian, Flemish and Breton mercenaries fought for William in his campaign against his southern neighbor, Count Elias of Maine. The money for these troops came from England where it had been raised by Ranulph. William's commander in this Maine campaign was given large sums of money to purchase soldiers, including those crossbowmen, archers and engineers who played a crucial role in the siege and capture of LeMans.

William was able to maintain himself on the throne and extend his continental possessions through his use of hired warriors. It is not surprising, therefore, that when he died in 1100 he was described as a man "beloved by the mercenaries for his numerous gifts, but unlamented by the people because he brought about the plundering of their property." [9]

The year 1100 is important not only for Henry's coronation, which took place in August, but also for Robert's return from the Holy Land the following month. With Curthose's arrival in Normandy the separation of the duchy from the kingdom, which had been at the root of disloyalty since the Conqueror's death, resumed. That little had changed was shown by a rebellion against Henry I in 1101–02 which resembled that of 1088. Both revolts took place within a year of the accession of a new king, and aimed at making the Norman duke the English king; each was inspired by a Norman prelate who had been exiled from the island and was trying to regain his confiscated possessions; both saw leading barons of the English king defect to Duke Robert; and in both cases the king turned for support to mercenaries.

Once again many of the same baronial faces appeared in opposition to the King: the three sons of Roger of Montgomery, Robert, Roger and Arnulph; Eustace of Boulogne; Robert of Lacy. This time they were joined by William of Warrenne, son of yet another leading companion of the Conqueror. The revolt was inspired by Ranulph who had been imprisoned by Henry and escaped to Normandy. The Bishop of Durham convinced Robert that the time was ripe for a takeover of the island. Although Robert sailed to England in 1101 supported by many of Henry's barons, the disagreement between the brothers was settled by a treaty. Henry, upset by the participation of many of his lords in Robert's cause, called upon Robert of Bellême during the following year to answer in his court the charge of treason. With this summons began the last major revolt in England until the reign of Stephen. Robert of Bellême defied the king and prepared his castles for war. Henry's military campaign against the rebels lasted six months and required sieges of the castles of Arundel, Tickhill, Bridgnorth and Shrewsbury. Mercenaries, especially Welsh, were liberally employed by the King due to the length of the campaign, the number of sieges involved, and the doubtful loyalty of many of the lords. When the rebellion was crushed the huge Montgomery holdings were split and the sons of Roger sent into exile.

A peace that was to last for thirty-three years settled upon the island. This was due in part to the dispersal of the rebels and in part to Henry's defeat of Robert at Tinchebrai four years later. By this victory the King once again united Normandy and England and removed the main source of disloyalty from his kingdom—the system of double allegiances. In the battle at Tinchebrai Henry used Breton mercenaries who played a major role in the defeat of the Duke's army. After 1106 Normandy served as a military buffer shielding England from Henry's continental enemies. The English king continued to employ mercenaries on the Continent for the remainder of his reign. A battle at Alençon in 1118 was fought by hired soldiers. In the following year the English King defended his castle at Bures against Baldwin VII of Flanders with mercenaries. In 1123 he employed them to put down a revolt on behalf of William Clito. On this occasion hired troops captured the rebel leader, an action which gave Henry the victory.

Mercenaries were a feature of Henry's military forces, as they had been of his father's and brother's armies before him. These three Anglo-Norman kings set a precedent of hiring soldiers which was to be continued and improved upon by their successors. Between 1066 and 1135 the basic institutions to support a mercenary policy, such as an organized Exchequer and scutage, were begun. When the need to hire mercenaries became more pressing during the reigns of Stephen and Henry II, these monarchs found ready to hand the instruments necessary for such a policy.

*"A savage crowd of barbarians . . .
had swarmed to England in a body
to serve as mercenaries."*
———Gesta Stephani

CHAPTER IV

King Stephen

THE reign of King Stephen (1135–54), sometimes referred to as an interregnum by those orderly-minded historians who countenance no deviation from royal geneological tables, is often pictured as a nineteen-year institutional coma during which progress in the development of most English institutions was temporarily suspended. Perhaps there is a grain of justification for this view as applied to the Exchequer, the Pipe Rolls or the Chancellery, but for the institution of mercenaries there is none. On the contrary, the practice of hiring soldiers in lieu of feudal service gained momentum under Stephen, making this period one of direct continuity with the preceding reigns.

Two factors were primarily responsible for this increased use of mercenaries. In the first place, Stephen came to the throne as a rich and influential man. He had been one of the most important English barons during Henry's time and was well acquainted, as were the other English lords, with the practice of collecting scutage from his vassals and using the money to purchase substitutes. Not only was he one of the wealthiest men in the kingdom in his own right, but he added to his assets the immense treasury of Henry I soon after that king's death. And, unlike his predecessors, he had no scruples about confiscating Church revenues when the need for more fighting men arose. Secondly, the problem of disloyalty which had been serious enough with the Conqueror and his sons, blossomed into a full-scale civil war with Stephen, making it even more imperative that he find a regular, non-feudal source of military manpower. The result was to convert the hiring of mercenary soldiers from a practice into an institution. Evidence for this is found in the fact that during Stephen's reign military campaigns were longer and more frequent and sieges more common than before. All pretense of relying on a "feudal array" was abandoned as both sides purchased their military power. Stephen's ability to remain on the English throne until his death was due to the financial, rather than feudal, advantage he enjoyed over his enemies.

Stephen's financial potential was already very much in evidence before his "election" in 1135. Long before then he was recognized as a man of great wealth and prestige. The source of both lay in his widespread possessions on both sides of the Channel. As a favorite of his uncle, Henry I, he received the large revenue producing fiefs of Mortain, Boulogne, Eye and Lancaster—possessions which had propelled him to a prominent position in Anglo-Norman society.

Stephen began to build his financial empire in 1106 with the acquisition of the Norman county of Mortain. This gift he obtained from Henry I as a reward for his participation in the battle of Tinchebrai. That Mortain was a prestigious possession—a medieval status symbol—can be inferred from the list of important figures who possessed it, both before and after Stephen's time. In 1066 William the Conqueror bestowed it upon his half-brother, Robert, one of the ten most important landholders of the Anglo-Norman period. Upon Stephen's death in 1154 Mortain went to his son William who kept it for the remaining six years of his life. Henry II at that time thought highly enough of the county to allow it to return to the Crown and paid Matthew of Boulogne an annual £1000 to be rid of the latter's claim to the territory. Matthew thought it was worth even more since he deserted Henry the elder and his pension in 1173 and sided with his son, the young Henry, who held out Mortain to him as a reward for his support against his father. Near the end of the century the county was given to John by his royal brother, Richard the Lion-Hearted. Great value must indeed have been attached to this county which for a century and a half continued either among the possessions of the royal family or as a diplomatic pawn.

A revealing incident during Stephen's reign supports this. In 1141 the King fell briefly into the hands of his enemy, the Empress Matilda. The disposal of Mortain became the source of serious contention between the Empress and Stephen's influential brother, Bishop Henry of Winchester. Matilda's adamant refusal to allow Henry to confer the county upon the incarcerated king's son, Eustace, alienated the Bishop and, along with him, the Church. One chronicler branded this decision "the origin of all the evils that followed in England." [1]

In addition to prestige, Mortain was worth about thirty knights —or their equivalent—to Stephen. This was its value in 1172, and the static nature of the other Norman honors between 1135 and 1172 suggests no change in Mortain during the intervening period. This figure places the county among the important and influential honors of Normandy and its possessor among the leading barons.

Another of Stephen's possessions was Boulogne which came to him through his wife Matilda, the daughter of Eustace, Count of Boulogne. When his father-in-law died Stephen inherited the title and territories of the continental county. The importance of this county lay more in its English manors than in the continental land itself. These included land in at least twelve counties. Although centered in Essex it spread into Oxford, Hampshire, Somerset, Hertfordshire, Suffolk, Kent, Surrey, Bedfordshire, Cambridgeshire, Huntingdon and Norfolk. All of these manors, together valued at over one hundred knights' fees, were securely in Stephen's hands before he became king.

Two other fiefs of importance had already come to Stephen as a result of baronial disloyalty toward Henry I and his uncle's munificence toward him. The honor of Eye, in Suffolk, was forfeited by Robert Malet in 1106 and given to Stephen. It comprised about 250 manors and was valued at eighty knights' fees in 1166. But Stephen's largest single possession was the honor of Lancaster, situated mostly in the northern part of England. During Robert of Bellême's abortive rebellion against Henry I in 1102, his brother Roger forfeited his extensive holdings as the price for having joined Robert. These possessions included manors in Suffolk, Lincolnshire, Nottinghamshire, and vast but barren lands in the northwestern part of the kingdom. Stephen received them some time between 1115 and 1118. In 1172 the honor of Lancaster was valued at sixty-eight and one-half knights' fees, which was probably less than it was worth when Stephen held it. In the Pipe Roll of

1130 Stephen appears as a landholder in seventeen of the twenty-eight counties listed. In that same year he was excused from payment of Danegeld totalling £199 8s. which represented about ten percent of the entire remittance. All of this shows that Stephen possessed a solid financial base prior to his elevation to the English throne.

Although Stephen's own possessions were valuable and of great military potential, the thing that caught the eye and imagination of contemporary chroniclers was his seizure of Henry's wealth immediately after his coronation in 1135. A contemporary placed the value of the treasury as it passed into Stephen's hands at £100,000 in cash, plus an inestimable amount in gold and silver vessels. In addition, Stephen took over a realm that was in sound financial condition. The one surviving Pipe Roll from Henry's reign shows an income to the Crown in 1130 of £66,593. At the time of Henry's death the annual royal revenues were high enough and the treasury full enough to evoke awesome descriptions from the chroniclers and to provide Stephen the wherewithal to purchase mercenaries.

That he did so, and on a large scale, is evident from the sources. Hired forces, usually Flemings, figured prominently in every major military engagement of the reign, with the exception of the Battle of the Standard in 1138. It has been suggested that these Flemings were supplied by the Count of Flanders through the money fief known to have been arranged earlier between Henry I and the Flemish count. This was impossible on several counts. In the first place the Flemish ruler, Thierry of Alsace, was an enemy of Stephen and a supporter of the Empress Matilda. Furthermore, throughout the first decade of Stephen's reign Thierry was militarily occupied against his neighbor, Baldwin of Hainault. After 1146 the Flemish count and his soldiers were occupied with the Second Crusade, toward which they directed all available manpower and resources. There were no knights left over to send to England. Again, the complete silence of the Flemish chroniclers concerning the presence in England of knights of their county is testimony to their absence there. The final piece of evidence is the most telling. The Flemings who fought for Stephen were under the command of the mercenary captain, William of Ypres, who was a personal friend of the King and enemy of the Flemish count. William had been refused the countship of Flanders in 1127 and fled to England in the wake of Thierry's rise to power there two years later. The Flemings he led in Stephen's cause were not supplied by the Flemish count but were hired soldiers, probably dispossessed by the civil wars and anarchy that swept through their native land during the reign of Henry I in England.

Thus Stephen possessed the money and personnel to permit him to hire mercenaries. The third ingredient, a motive, was supplied by the presence of organized opposition, both legal and military, to his kingship. In the Anglo-Norman days before 1135, disloyalty had resulted in sporadic rebellions against the king and the halting use of mercenaries. The existence now of a counter-claimant to the throne, the Empress Matilda, brought about an infinitely greater display of disunity and the regularization of the employment of hired soldiers by Stephen. Organized, strategic opposition to Stephen reached its height in the middle decade of his reign, 1139–49 and, although the King's use of mercenaries was not restricted to that period, it was then that they performed their greatest service.

In many ways Stephen's first year was a microcosm of his entire reign. The disunity and reliance on mercenaries which were to become so patent after 1139 were prefigured at the outset. In 1136 the King countered a Scottish invasion from the north during February and March, Welsh raids from March through October, and major revolts in the southeast in April and in the southwest throughout the summer. These two latter revolts were early indications of the later alliance between the extreme western and eastern portions of the kingdom which would form the theater for the civil war. In 1136 mercenaries were used against the Welsh and against the rebels in Devonshire.

The uprising in the southeast was led by Hugh Bigod, a power in Norfolk and Suffolk, who armed the castle of Norwich against Stephen. Even though he surrendered the stronghold to the King without a siege, he remained a thorn in Stephen's side and later sided with the Empress. Contemporaries spoke of him as "the most restless opponent" of the king [2] and "an inveterate enemy of the king's cause." [3]

At the other end of the kingdom, in Devonshire, Baldwin of Redwers defied the King by fortifying the castle of Exeter. It took

Stephen the entire summer, from June to September, to win the castle back. He did so with the aid of mercenary archers, slingers and miners. Although the King pardoned Baldwin, the latter fled to the Isle of Wight. Stephen followed with his army and forced Baldwin's final surrender at Southampton.

Thus during 1136 Stephen's army, or at least sizeable segments of it, were in the field almost continuously from February through October. Feudal and militia resources were not designed for such prolonged activity. The logistical problem alone of dovetailing several thousand forty- or sixty-day service periods would tax even the computerized manpower management procedures of a modern army. Mercenaries appear to have been the only solution to the problem.

Even more important for the future was a decision made that same year by Robert, Earl of Gloucester and half-brother of the Empress Matilda. Robert had been absent from the coronation the previous year and had also missed Stephen's first Easter court early in 1136. He remained in Normandy trying to resolve the dilemma presented on the one hand by an oath he had taken to uphold his sister's claim to the throne, and on the other by Stephen's *de facto* possession of the English crown. Furthermore, the Earl was greatly upset by Stephen's use of Henry's treasure to surround himself with hired soldiers and bodyguards. When he finally came to England in April and swore his oath to the new King, Robert did so conditionally, and only for the purpose of gaining admission to Stephen's council to subvert it, not to support it. Having decided that open resistance to Stephen's mercenary policy would be fruitless, he hoped to convince the barons of the error they had made in supporting Stephen and of the necessity of their returning to feudal decency, which involved placing Matilda on the throne.

Robert's plan met with little success and he was forced to abandon it the following year. A series of incidents during a campaign in Normandy in 1137 caused Robert to drop all pretense of loyalty and to begin gathering support against Stephen. Once again the earl's decision resulted from the presence of mercenaries in Stephen's army. At the urging of his mercenary captain, William of Ypres, the King tried to ambush Robert as he landed in Normandy. Although Robert frustrated the plot, he conveyed his

resentment of the King's mercenary policy to the English and
Norman lords who were supporting the King's campaign. During
a march against Geoffrey of Anjou this jealousy flared up and fighting broke out between Stephen's feudal and mercenary elements.
The King was forced to halt the campaign and treat with the
Angevin count. Robert openly espoused his sister's cause of which
he remained the leader until his death in 1147.

Now it became the King's turn to resolve a dilemma. His
mercenary army, originally created as a counterweight to disloyalty, was becoming a cause of it. As baronial defection spread
the need for mercenaries to offset it grew larger; but the increase
in the number of hired soldiers resulted in even stronger opposition
from the feudal contingent. This became more apparent in 1138
when, as a result of Robert's open break with Stephen, many important barons representing both eastern and western shires, deserted the King for Matilda. Sides were being chosen for the civil
war which was but one year away, and Stephen had no choice
but to rely even more heavily upon his hired forces.

While the southern tenants were jockeying for position, a new
threat swept in from the north. Beginning early in 1138 David,
King of the Scots, staged three invasions of England before he was
finally defeated in August near Northallerton. Stephen was per-
sonally involved only in the first raid, and then only for a short
period of time. There is no direct indication in the abundant literature of these campaigns that mercenaries were used against the
northern King. The defense of England was left to those most immediately threatened, the northern barons. They appeared at the
Battle of the Standard in August with "their men," warriors who
otherwise remain faceless. It has already been noted, however, that
by this time the English lords were acquainted with the practice of
collecting scutage from their vassals and hiring mercenaries to replace them. It is conceivable that the archers and foot soldiers who
performed so splendidly against the Scots on this occasion were
paid for their military service.

Stephen's use of mercenaries against the Welsh and Scots and
in strengthening his own position against rebellious barons had, by
1139, made serious inroads into his treasury. Having cast his lot with
a mercenary policy, he was in need of a new source of revenue to

finance it. The King's predecessors had, for the most part, left the lands of the Church alone, preferring to tap other feudal rights for money. But their need to pay soldiers' salaries nowhere approached that of Stephen. In 1139 the King made his move against the richest Church lands in the realm. He arrested Roger, Bishop of Salisbury and his two nephews, the Bishops of Lincoln and Ely, and confiscated their eight castles.

Mercenaries were involved in virtually every step of Stephen's operation against the bishops. Their arrest was touched off by a fight between some of Roger's knights and a few of Alan of Dinant's mercenaries. When Nigel, Bishop of Ely fled to Devizes to avoid imprisonment, the mercenary William of Ypres was sent to apprehend him.

This was a momentous step and the King's motives were mixed. Undoubtedly Stephen's suspicion that the castles were being readied for the Empress and her brother played a role in his decision. However, the obvious note of satisfaction and feigned surprise with which one of the chroniclers describes the enormous caches of arms and money found in Roger's castles [4] suggests that the King viewed the seizure as a way out of his financial problem. The possessions of the Bishop of Salisbury, which could only be described as magnificent, had attracted the impoverished King's attention and their seizure rapidly and efficiently replenished Stephen's wealth "just after he had drained his own treasuries almost to exhaustion to protect his kingdom." [5]

Perhaps another motive was at work—also involved with the question of mercenaries. Those fighters able to sell their martial abilities in the twelfth century were, for the most part, men who existed outside the mainstream of society. They had no feudal ties to constrain them and were unbound by normal social obligations. During periods of unemployment they roamed the countryside, terrorizing defenseless peasants, sacking churches and monasteries and, in general, disrupting the peace of Europe. In the latter part of the eleventh century the Church initiated a concentrated campaign to pacify Europe. The First Crusade, preached in 1095, was partly an attempt to drain Europe of some of its warring elements. The Truce and Peace of God looked in the same direction. The Church had declared war on brigands and unattached mercenaries, and many of its councils, from the lowest diocesan level to Rome itself, anathematized these outlaws. Just two months before Stephen's move against the bishops in England the Lateran Council adopted a canon excommunicating archers and crossbowmen, labeling them as hateful in the sight of God, and prohibiting Christian rulers from employing them. This pronouncement threatened Stephen's mercenary policy and represented a repetition from the pulpit of that very criticism levelled at him by his lay barons. The pleas of the Archbishop of Canterbury that the King restore the bishops fell on deaf ears. Even had he wished to do so, Stephen could not abandon his mercenaries at this point. The rapid advance of events had forced his hand.

The military phase of the civil war began with the arrival of Matilda in England in the fall of 1139. It has been suggested that the tales of the subsequent devastation and ruin throughout the island have been greatly exaggerated coming, as they did, from the pens of chroniclers who were knowledgeable only about their own local area and who tended to generalize from this limited information. An examination of the widespread support enjoyed by Matilda suggests otherwise. Shortly after her arrival a large block of southwestern counties consolidated behind the Empress. In addition to Gloucestershire, she received support from Devonshire, Cornwall, Somerset, Dorsetshire, Herefordshire and much of Wiltshire. These counties alone had accounted for one-fourth of the total enfeoffments of the realm four years earlier. Additional sympathy for Matilda came from the northern counties of Chester and Northumberland, the central shires of Huntingdon and Northampton, and the eastern part of the country, especially in Norfolk and Suffolk. When to this is added the loss of Church support, it becomes obvious that the war was truly civil and widespread, and it is understandable that the King employed paid warriors.

Although civil war and divided allegiance continued until 1153, and military action in support of it remained relatively constant until the Empress' departure from the island in 1148, the most decisive and dramatic episodes occurred between 1140 and 1143. Mercenaries were used by both sides, and virtually every military decision, as well as several diplomatic ones, were a result of their presence. Stephen's military problem was to prevent the Empress from uniting her eastern and western allies. Most of the King's activity in these years took place in the Thames Valley, with frequent excursions westward to divide the rebels under Robert of Gloucester, and eastward to mop up pockets of resistance in Norfolk and Suffolk. An itinerary of Stephen's movements shows him constantly on the move, devoting the larger part of each year to campaigning. The majority of these actions featured sieges. Although many of these were directed against weak or lightly defended castles, and therefore of short duration, there were enough lengthy ones to suggest a heavy reliance on hired soldiers.

The most critical actions took place in 1141 and 1142 and centered around the strongholds of Lincoln, Winchester and Oxford. As a result of Stephen's success in these two years, the rebel forces were to remain permanently divided east and west. Early in 1141, while besieging the castle of Lincoln, Stephen was captured by Robert of Gloucester. His mercenaries occupied tactically important positions during the battle. William of Ypres commanded the Flemish mercenaries on the left, and the mercenary Alan of Dinant was in charge of the right. It was the flight of these two wings that led to Stephen's capture. Had these hired troops been small in number or in positions of relative unimportance the King might have remained free. This almost total reliance on mercenaries in such a key battle further suggests the paucity of Stephen's feudal following.

With the capture of the King most of the remaining feudal forces went over to the Empress. Even the King's brother, Henry, proclaimed his neutrality and began to speak of the Empress as "the first lady of the English." [6] The greater part of the kingdom came under her sway. Only the queen, William of Ypres and his mercenaries, and the county of Kent remained faithful to the captured monarch. Kent's adherence was probably due to the fact that William of Ypres held extensive lands in the shire. Although this was the lowpoint in Stephen's fortunes, it was at this very time that his military policy was vindicated and that his original assessment of the potential disloyalty of the feudality and the inherent weakness of the system of knight-service proved to be correct. Had it not been for the constancy of his mercenaries and their subsequent performance at the siege of Winchester later in the year, Stephen's reign would have ended in February 1141.

Henry of Winchester's flirtation with the rebels was short-lived. Disillusioned by the Empress he returned to his brother's cause and in mid-summer began the siege of the castle of Winchester, then held by the Angevin forces. William of Ypres and his mercenaries joined the bishop and proved their worth by destroying the forces of John the Marshal and capturing Robert of Gloucester. The seizure of the Earl, and his subsequent exchange for King Stephen, restored the realm to its pre-Lincoln condition. It was to remain virtually unchanged until the death of Stephen thirteen years later.

Although the strategic situation remained static during the rest of Stephen's reign, there were significant tactical activities involving mercenaries. Stephen spent the greater part of 1142 campaigning on the island. From June through December he was present at the sieges of Wareham, Cirencester, Bampton, Radcot and Oxford. This final one lasted three months and ended shortly after Christmas with the capitulation of the castle and the flight of the Empress. In the summer of 1143 Stephen used his Flemish mercenaries in an unsuccessful attempt to defend the town of Wilton against Robert. During the following year the King was occupied from the spring through September in the fenland around the Isle of Ely. His quarry was Geoffrey of Mandeville, descendant of one of the Conqueror's leading companions. Geoffrey had changed sides several times in the civil war. Stephen had arrested him the previous September and seized his strategic castles, whereupon Geoffrey fled to the fens of Ely and began a reign of terror against the inhabitants. The length of Stephen's campaign against him, plus the guerrilla nature of the war, suggest that the King's mercenaries played an important role. Geoffrey's death in September ended the campaign and the threat from the east. Stephen was fortunate in having the luxury of being able to concentrate on one enemy at a time. Following the defeat at Oxford, the Empress' forces retreated to Bristol where Robert set up a lordship, collected scutage, and, in imitation of the King, recruited mercenaries. These activities occupied him throughout most of 1143 and 1144, permitting Stephen to concentrate on Geoffrey.

The war continued after the death of Geoffrey of Mandeville in 1144 but in a desultory fashion. The pace quickened on three occasions, in 1147, 1149 and 1153. In each of these years the

Empress' son, Henry of Anjou, tried his hand against Stephen by invading England at the head of a band of mercenaries. Henry's campaign of 1153 was the largest and the only decisive one of the three. He landed in January with over one hundred knights and three thousand infantrymen, probably mercenaries. Stephen opposed him with hired soldiers and the campaign dragged on into November. A settlement finally was reached by a treaty at Winchester between the King and the Duke of Anjou. Stephen was permitted to retain the throne until his death, at which time Henry was to receive the crown.

The terms of the treaty of Winchester are indicative of the value placed by both sides on mercenaries. Two military measures were agreed upon to insure the pacification of England. The first was the destruction of all castles that had been constructed without the King's permission. The second was the expulsion of mercenaries from the island. It was hoped that the removal of these two most important military elements would bring about the much sought after peace. Even though the realization of both measures had to await the accession of Henry the following year, this does not diminish the fact that in the view of contemporary commanders there would be no warfare without castles and hired soldiers.

Stephen's use of mercenaries trailed off in these waning years of his reign only because there was a slackening of military activity. Such military action as there was saw their use by both sides, but this was sporadic. Both sides were war-weary and a stalemate resulted. The leading chronicler of the period complains of the devastations caused by "a savage crowd of barbarians, who swarmed to England in a body to serve as mercenaries," but were now no longer in the hire of their former paymasters.[7] It would seem that the years of conflict had rendered large portions of England valueless to their owners, thereby curtailing the potential for the purchase of soldiers. This was surely true for the King, and the chronicler implies the same to be the case for the rebels. The inability of either side to purchase soldiers ground the military machinery to a halt—an indication of the importance of mercenaries in twelfth-century warfare.

Mercenaries, therefore, were of primary importance during the reign of Stephen. Lacking any other long-serving alternative to knight-service, and possessing the money and motive to hire mercenaries, the King transformed into a policy a practice of his predecessors. To a large degree this mercenary policy was forced upon him by the inherent weakness of the existing military system which was unworkable when anything less than full loyalty to the monarch was present. It is impossible to determine with any degree of accuracy the number of mercenaries involved. It has been estimated that the band of Flemings recruited and led by William of Ypres on Stephen's behalf included about three hundred souls. What is certain is that their numbers increased in proportion to the decrease in reliability of the feudal barons and knights. A scant two generations after its purported introduction into England, the system of knight-service, which was designed to supply the ruler with the requisite amount of military support, was incapable of doing so. Stephen's need to rely on hired soldiers clearly shows that if the system of knight-service—which has become synonymous with the term "feudalism"—ever did operate as fully in practice as called for by the theory, that day had passed before the twelfth century had run half its course.

*"Being unwilling to inconvenience the
knights furnished by the landed
barons. . . . He took with him a
countless host of hired soldiers."*
——— Robert of Torigni

CHAPTER V

Henry Plantagenet

HENRY PLANTAGENET'S reign (1154–89) appears on the surface to differ little from that of Stephen with respect to the frequency with which military forces were hired. Statistically speaking, Henry's dependence on mercenaries was every bit as total as had been that of his predecessor. The reasons behind the mercenary policy, however, were different in each case. Stephen hired soldiers to compensate for the feudal losses he suffered through disunity and civil war. Henry likewise lost the military support of his barons, but not as a result of disloyalty and war. Quite the contrary. The Angevin king's decision to hire mercenaries resulted from the long period of peace which the island enjoyed during his reign. With the civil war behind them, the war-weary nobility of England welcomed the opportunity to return to peaceful pursuits. The result was a resumption of institution building which the war had interrupted. Henry gave his barons full rein in this direction, and was energetic in associating them in the task of constructing diversified departments of government. During his reign the Exchequer, royal courts, travelling justices and sheriffdoms took a giant step in the direction of becoming bureaucratized. This division of the royal household into specialized departments required an expansion of personnel. The bodies to man these departments came mainly from among the nobility.

Governmental bureaucratic institutions increased not only in size but also in sophistication during the second half of the twelfth century. There was a need not only for more people, but for more specialized people, to run the country. As a result the energies of the tenants-in-chief were gradually diverted toward administrative labors and away from the pursuits of war. The King encouraged this. From his military experience in England during Stephen's reign he had learned the advantages of hiring fighters and using the barons to help him raise money to pay them by converting feudal dues into hard cash. By employing his lords in this manner, and using mercenaries in times of war, he was able to ward off many of the problems with the nobility which his predecessors had faced. The extension and organization of revenues produced sufficient funds from ordinary sources with which to pay his soldiers. He was not forced, for example, to dip into Church revenues as Stephen had done. The problem of disloyalty arose only once in England, and then towards the end of the reign, by which time his mercenary forces were more than adequate to handle it. In his battles with forces outside the kingdom he was not plagued with the problem of short-term enlistments and the departure of his warriors after forty days. Mercenaries fought as long as the paycheck was guaranteed. In short, Henry used mercenaries as a result of peaceful conditions in England; his dependence on them in turn strengthened that very peace.

One of Henry's first acts was to expel from England the Flemish mercenaries that had been employed by both sides during the civil war. The chroniclers made a big issue of this, implying that Henry was wholly against the idea of mercenaries. A closer look at this decision, however, suggests that Henry was not opposed to mercenaries *per se*. In the first place, not all the mercenaries left the island. William of Ypres was allowed to remain in possession of his Kentish possessions, and apparently it was not until 1157 that he returned to Flanders to retire to the monastery of St. Peter at Loo. This same leniency was extended to some of his Flemish followers who were permitted to stay in England on condition that they retire to Pembrokeshire. Furthermore, he had made an agreement with Stephen at Winchester the year before his accession to rid the island of mercenaries. In view of the personal nature of medieval kingship, and the necessity of winning the support of the barons, it would have been suicidal for any monarch to begin his reign by breaking the very promise that was responsible for his elevation to the throne. In addition, the non-English mercenaries upon whom Henry depended throughout his reign were used almost exclusively outside England, so that their expulsion at this time had little effect on his overall policy. Finally, as we shall see, Henry made little use of Flemings. His hired troops were drawn mainly from Brabant and Wales. The expulsion of the Flemings in 1154, therefore, was a tactical rather than a strategic move, and is not indicative of his general policy of hiring soldiers.

This monarch's dependence on paid soldiery in his continental campaigns has always been recognized. What has been less patent was Henry's implementation of the same policy in England. Bishop Stubbs set the tone for this discussion over a century ago with his remark that "the obvious policy (of Henry II) was to use mercenaries for foreign warfare and to employ the national militia for defense and the maintenance of peace." [1] Since there was only one significant military action on the island throughout the entire reign we cannot depend solely on the chroniclers, who recorded mostly the dramatic, to tell us about the forces used by Henry to keep his kingdom in a state of ready defense. Fortunately evidence of a different kind becomes dependable precisely at this time—the annual financial accounts of the sheriffs. These Pipe Rolls, as they are called, provide invaluable information concerning the inner workings of the kingdom. They show that during Henry's time there existed a structure of paid personnel responsible for the maintenance of peace and the defense of the island. Their duties included the manning of castles, the preparation and distribution of the materials of war and, when required, participation in combat. The fact that they were seldom called upon to perform in actual combat in no way detracts from the fact that they were mercenaries, paid for their martial abilities.

These same Pipe Rolls also clearly show how and where Henry obtained the money he needed to pay his soldiers. Most of it came from the commutation of military service through the collection of scutage. For the first time we are able to speak in detail about this important institution. Henry used it on seven occasions, each one in conjunction with a major military campaign.

In addition to telling us how the money was collected, the Pipe Rolls also indicate where the money was spent. There are scores of references throughout its pages to payments for military materiel and personnel, in time of peace as well as in time of war. They lead to the conclusion that Henry bought the defense of his island.

Henry passed twenty of his thirty-five royal years on the Continent. It was there that the focus of his empire lay, and it was in defense of his French lands that he engaged in his many military campaigns. England took on the aspect of a large treasury to support his continental policy. Since Henry spent most of his time and money across the Channel we will look first to the use of mercenaries in these campaigns. A discussion of the importance of hired forces in England itself will be deferred till later.

Henry's first continental war was fought in 1156 when his brother Geoffrey claimed title to the counties of Anjou, Maine and Touraine. The campaign lasted the first five months of the year, and ended with the King's capture of his brother's three castles at Chinon, Mirabeau and Loudon. A scutage of approximately £2230 was raised in England for this war, and the money was transferred to the Continent by one William Cumin who received a salary of seventeen shillings for his effort. None of the castles surrendered without a fight. Henry's need to besiege them, coupled with the length of the campaign, made it imperative that mercenaries be used. The financial returns of that year from Middlesex and Gloucestershire show that those counties paid the salary of soldiers from Wallingford and Hereford who joined the King.

In the following year Henry led his army into Wales where he forced the submission of Owen, a local king in the northern part of that country. No general scutage was collected in England for this campaign. Some of the barons, however, bought their way out of the fighting. The Abbot of Abbotsbury, for example, paid a scutage of two marks during the year, for the "Welsh expedition." Robert of Torigni says that the entire feudal host was called upon to participate. According to him, this was done in such a way that every two knights supplied and equipped a third. This arrangement could have been a variety of scutage whereby the type of participation required was financial. The guerrilla nature of warfare against the Welsh in the mountainous and wooded terrain of the country suggests the use of unmounted fighters, not the cumbersome cavalry of the supposed feudal array. Archers figured prominently in the campaign, and they were paid from the revenues of Shropshire. The royal treasury was removed to Wales for the occasion and, although it is not unusual to find the treasury accompanying the king in the Middle Ages, its presence at the scene of a military campaign is suggestive of the presence of mercenaries.

In August 1158 Henry returned to the Continent for a stay of over four years. Three scutages were collected during these years, each to support the monarch's military activity abroad. The first, in 1159, was the largest of the reign,[2] and was used to finance Henry's campaign against Toulouse that same year. Although Henry was accompanied on this sally into southern France by "all the lords and barons of England, Normandy, Aquitaine, Anjou and Gascony," the feudal vassals of these tenants-in-chief were missing. Their absence and replacements were explained by the chronicler:

> And so king Henry, when he was about to set out on this expedition, out of regard for the length and difficulty of the journey, being unwilling to inconvenience the knights furnished by the landed barons, as well as the multitude of the towns-people and the rustics, received from the Normans a contribution of sixty shillings of money of Anjou from each knight's fee. . . . He took with him a countless host of hired soldiers and those barons who held of him *in capite*.[3]

This passage sheds light on the main features of Henry's mercenary policy. The generally peaceful aspect of the empire, the decay of martial spirit among the feudal knights and the militia, and the use of scutage to hire mercenaries are all clearly in evidence. The monarch's hesitancy to "inconvenience" the feudal host implies that the knights were unaccustomed to being diverted from their peaceful pursuits and that this situation predated the Toulouse campaign.

The Pipe Roll of this year comes alive with entries indicating the use of mercenaries against Toulouse. In addition to the general scutage, mercenary wages were paid in some cases directly by the counties and cities of England. For example, soldiers from Hereford were paid from the London revenues. Welsh mercenaries drew their pay from Buckinghamshire. Other references to the payment of mercenary salaries appear in the accounts from Norfolk, Suffolk, Kent and Devonshire.

The campaign was a failure. After three months of activity, two of which were spent in besieging Toulouse, Henry broke it off and returned to Normandy. That duchy then became his base of operations against the French king for the next three years. In 1160 Henry besieged and took the castle of Chaumont-sur-Loire to prevent it from falling into the hands of King Louis. In 1161 open warfare between the two monarchs was barely avoided on two occasions. Each time both kings appeared accompanied by their full military complements. Military and administrative demands kept Henry on the Continent until January 1163. Such prolonged military operations overseas could hardly have been sustained without the support of mercenaries. They were paid through the collection of two scutages during the period, one in 1161, the other in 1162. As in 1159, the scutage money was supplemented by payments to mercenaries from many of the English counties. In 1161, for instance, sailors at Southampton received £100 in salary from the proceeds of Hampshire. A London return of the same year earmarked over £21 for the purchase of shields for mercenaries.

In 1165 Henry was back in Wales for another try at subduing the restless Welsh kings. Once again he resorted to a general scutage to finance the expedition, and the sum collected was slightly over £2000. Preparations for this campaign had been made at Northampton the preceding October. Heavy feudal horsemen being ineffective against the highly mobile, light-armed Welsh, it was decided that each tenant would pay, in addition to the scutage, the salary of one mercenary for six months. Besides native English hired soldiers, many Flemings and Danes were imported to fight against the Welsh. The campaign, which lasted from May to August, took place in two phases, punctuated by a regrouping at Shrewsbury. In May the King marched along the northern coast of Wales to Rhuddlan, only to find that the Welsh had retreated down the heavily forested Clwyd valley. Realizing that he would have to attack them from the south, Henry fortified his northern castles and returned to Shrewsbury to prepare his army for the southern campaign. June and July were spent at the Shropshire city marshalling mercenary troops and equipment. The extent of this logistical exercise is reflected in the Pipe Rolls, which mention money spent on salaries, uniforms, shields, arrows, battle axes and transportation for the King's mercenaries. As before, much of this was paid from shire revenues.

When the preparations were complete, the army marched through Oswestry to the Berwyn mountain range, harassed along the way by Welsh snipers. At the base of the mountain the rainy weather forced Henry to abandon the campaign and retreat to England. Despite its failure, the Welsh campaign provides a significant illustration of Henry's dependence on mercenaries. A by-product of this campaign was a contingent of Welsh mercenaries which Henry brought back to England. From this time on these Welsh appear as a regular feature alongside Henry's other hired soldiers.

Following the Berwyn disaster, Henry returned to Normandy for another four-year stay. As with his earlier visit, this sojourn on the Continent was occasioned by growing discontent among some of his vassals. King Louis of France took advantage of this situation to put pressure on Henry's lands. The French king aimed ultimately at taking Normandy itself from Henry, and to serve this purpose had fortified several castles on the Norman-French frontier, including Chaumont. In 1167 Henry decided upon the destruction of Chaumont and chose his newly organized band of Welsh mercenaries to perform the mission. The success of this venture was attributed by contemporaries to these paid soldiers. In May Henry left Gisors and marched up to the walls of Chaumont. His mercenaries swam a river which flowed past the castle, and set fire to the fortification while the French were making a foray. The capitulation of Chaumont ended for the time being Louis' attempt to take Normandy. The scene shifted to the southern possessions of the English monarch. Until a peace arrangement made with Louis in 1170, Henry spent most of his time putting down small rebellions among his vassals who were spurred on by the French monarch. Although direct evidence pointing to the use of mercenaries in these campaigns is lacking, the extended nature of the expeditions, together with the ready availability of fighters willing to sell their services, suggests that hired troops played a role in keeping Henry's continental possessions out of the hands of the monarch's enemies. No scutage was collected during these years. On the other hand, none of Henry's military activity was on a scale large enough to require exceptional expenditures. Mercenaries could well have been paid from the normal revenues of the Crown.

Scutage was collected again in 1171, this time for an expedition to Ireland. Problems had cropped up in that country while Henry was occupied in France. In 1166 Dermot McMurrough, the Irish king, was exiled from his island and sought Henry's assistance in his bid to regain the throne. The English king, preoccupied with his wars on the Continent, instructed some of his barons in western England to help the exile recover his land. A series of baronial expeditions to Ireland began in 1169. The most important of these was one recruited and led by Richard of Clare, the Earl of Striguil and Pembroke, more popularly known as "Strongbow." The Earl's motives were not entirely altruistic. His extravagant nature had led him to live beyond his means with the result that by 1170 he had dissipated a once sizeable inheritance and was being hounded by his creditors. Strongbow was neither the first nor last man in history to seek relief from his debts by going abroad. For the expedition he recruited Welsh mercenaries who likewise were moved by the prospect of regaining lost fortunes or adding to present ones.

Strongbow landed in Ireland in August, 1170, with a force of two hundred knights and one thousand light-armed mercenaries. He realized immediate success by capturing Waterford and Dublin and returning to Dermot many of his former possessions. When Dermot died the following May Strongbow had himself installed on the Irish throne. Henry, meanwhile, had been occupied in Normandy and with the Becket affair and was not free until August, 1171 to turn his attention to Irish matters. Although he had originally encouraged the expeditions of his barons to Ireland, the presence of one of them on the Irish throne was a different matter. Upon his return to England he set about collecting an army with which to impress the new "king" and insure his allegiance to the English crown. The mustering point for the army was Pembroke, and most of the forces gathered there were mercenaries. Scutage was levied on all tenants-in-chief who did not accompany the king to Ireland and the large number of contributors suggests that the number of knights who followed the king was small indeed. It has been suggested that the English fyrd, or militia, was used, but since this military arm was traditionally restricted to service within the realm, its presence at the Welsh expedition seems unlikely. As with the earlier Welsh campaign in 1165, the type of equipment gathered at Pembroke is indicative of the type of soldier employed. An entry in the London account of that year shows the payment of £78 for the repair of garments for 163 mercenaries who served the king in Ireland. Contemporary accounts stressed the fact that the two essential ingredients for the Irish expedition were Henry's troops and Henry's treasure—an indication that the latter was used to procure the former.

Henry accomplished his mission in Ireland short of military engagement. His appearance at the head of such a formidable array impressed not only the Earl of Pembroke, who ceded all his conquered territory to the monarch, but also many of the local Irish leaders who likewise did homage to the King. This represents no less a victory for Henry's mercenary policy than had actual military engagements taken place.

Henry's mercenary policy faced its most severe test when his sons rebelled against him in 1173–74 and joined Louis of France against their father. The English monarch was threatened simultaneously with the loss of his lands on the Continent and civil war at home. Since this was the only serious threat from within England during Henry's reign, the important part played by mercenaries in countering it is a significant indication of his reliance on hired forces to defend the island. Since the island phase of the revolt of 1173–74 is important in another context the discussion of it will be postponed. Of interest at the moment is the series of five major engagements which accompanied the revolt abroad. During the first year the English monarch overcame, in turn, an invasion from the north by the Count of Flanders, a siege of Verneuil by the French king, and a revolt in Brittany to the south. In 1174 he took the offensive in a campaign through Maine, Anjou and Touraine in the spring, and broke a siege of Rouen by Louis in mid-summer. In each case mercenaries spelled the difference between victory or defeat.

The war began shortly after Easter, 1173, when Philip of Flanders and Matthew of Boulogne, on behalf of the monarch's eldest son, Henry, invaded Normandy and seized a pair of castles in the northwestern corner of that duchy. Henry could rely only on northern mercenaries, the Brabantines, and transferred the royal treasury from England to Normandy to facilitate their hire. The invaders broke off the campaign and retreated to Flanders when Matthew was killed at Arques, but not before the French king, taking advantage of Henry's discomfiture, laid siege to Verneuil. This frontier castle, located due west of Paris and south of Rouen, was the gateway to Normandy from the east and its capture was a necessary prelude to an invasion of the duchy. Henry's castellans were able to hold off the French king through June and July, but as August approached their supplies dwindled and they were close to surrender. Early in August Henry, relieved of the northern threat, marched south from Rouen with a mercenary army and chased Louis back to France. The English army at this time contained Welsh mercenaries led by Richard, Earl of Pembroke, and the same Brabantines who had assisted Henry against the Flemings. One chronicler places the number of northern mercenaries at ten thousand—a figure which must not be taken literally, but should be interpreted to mean "a large number." King Henry relied upon mercenaries in this critical encounter because the Norman lords were occupied with the defense of their duchy against a reinvasion from the north.

No sooner had Henry returned to Rouen from Verneuil with his mercenaries than they had to march off in still another direction —this time southwest to Brittany. There a number of leading barons, egged on by Ralph of Fougères, had taken advantage of Henry's preoccupations in Normandy to seize the city of Dol. The chroniclers become almost lyric in describing the Brabantines' performance in this campaign, indicating that the only loyalty that could be depended upon at that time was that which was purchased. Once again, as in Normandy, the mercenaries were stronger than the rebels, and Brittany was rapidly returned to the King's side. The Brabantines met and quickly scattered Ralph's mounted and foot soldiers, many of whom were driven first into the castle at Dol and then into capitulation.

During May and June of 1174, Henry and his mercenaries roamed through the south, seizing rebel castles in Maine, Anjou and Poitou. While at Poitiers, the monarch learned that his son Richard had joined the revolt and captured the town of Saintes to the southwest. Henry's mercenaries took the town and secured the southern domains for the King. With the north, east, south and west quiet for the first time in over a year, Henry sailed with his mercenaries for England where it took him exactly one month— July 8–August 8—to end the revolt there. During his absence Louis again invaded Normandy and laid siege to the capital, Rouen. The English king flew back across the Channel with his Brabantine and Welsh mercenaries, the latter numbering about one thousand. This time it was the Welsh who were instrumental in breaking the siege. Being agile and accustomed to stealth, they sneaked through the woods and around the besiegers to intercept the French supply trains coming from Paris. Deprived of food the French were forced to lift the siege and retreat eastward. Soon afterwards Louis called for the first of several peace talks which led to a final settlement in September. The siege of Rouen was Louis' last attempt during the revolt to invade Normandy and its failure brought to an end the rebellion on the Continent. Looking at the continental revolt as a whole, each phase was met firmly by Henry and each of the rebel groups defeated by the forces which the English monarch had hired.

Scutage was not collected for these campaigns. Henry had by this time organized the Exchequer so that he was able to pay for his wars from the ordinary revenues of the realm. This is the implication of William of Newburgh's statement that the royal treasury provided the King with an abundant supply of ready money and was not to be spared in such an emergency. In addition, the King must have had some money left over from the previous year's expedition to Ireland which ended sooner than anticipated and without bloodshed. The presence of Strongbow and his Welsh mercenaries on the continent in 1173–74 suggests that the continental campaign was in some ways a continuation of the Irish campaign, 1171–72.

Henry's success with mercenaries against the rebels so increased his confidence in them that he placed the safety of his continental lands almost exclusively in their hands for the rest of his reign. Most of the trouble in these last years centered in Poitou and Aquitaine, which his son, Richard, administered for him. It was in these adolescent years that Richard, acting as his father's lieutenant, came to learn from personal experience the necessity and value of mercenaries. Later, as King and Crusader, the Lion-Hearted was to gain a widespread reputation as a military commander and employer of mercenaries.

Richard's continental adventures between 1175 and 1189 present a tableau of monotonously similar pictures. In 1175 he spent his father's money to hire mercenaries against rebels in Poitou, Saintonge, Limousin and Angoulême. Two years later he again led his mercenaries southward, this time as far as Gascony and the Pyrenees. He was joined in this campaign by Henry who crossed the Channel to assist his son in subduing the southern rebels. In 1178 Richard made good use of his hired troops in reducing the formidable castle at Taillebourg in Saintonge. Aquitaine was again the scene of unrest in 1181 and 1182, and Henry joined his son and his mercenaries in putting down the insurrection there. In 1183 Henry was challenged again by his eldest son, Henry, who led a league of nobles and mercenaries against Limoges. Richard sided with his father. He recruited mercenaries from Gascony under Raymond of Brun and recaptured the town and castle. The young Henry was forced to borrow twenty thousand sous from the burgesses of Limoges to pay his troops, and when this money ran out he seized the belongings of the Abbeys of St. Martial, Grandmont and Couronne. In this same campaign, Richard's mercenaries were responsible for the reduction of a strongly fortified castle of Bertrand of Born, one of the leading rebels. Although both sides used mercenaries, Henry II and Richard emerged the victors because they had had more experience with hired forces and held a recruiting advantage.

The revolts in southern France were finally crushed by Richard in 1187. The Pipe Rolls tell of Welsh mercenaries paid by and sent from the western shires of Shropshire and Hereford to fight alongside the King on the Continent. These fighters had been hired by Henry during the previous year for an anticipated expedition to Ireland—the sole major military adventure outside the Continent during the last decade of Henry's life. A scutage—the 'Great Scutage of Galway'—was collected and an army of mercenaries was mustered at Carlisle for the march into Ireland. War was avoided by the timely submission of the Irish rebel, Roland, at Carlisle. The presence of these Welsh mercenaries in Richard's army on the Continent during the following year, and the fact that they were paid by the same counties in 1187 as in 1186, suggests they were the same warriors.

Henry, therefore, had available during the final campaigns of his life two sources from which to draw mercenaries: France, both north and south, whence came a large number of drifting brigands; and Wales, whose footmen and archers became a regular part of the Plantagenet armies since Henry's Welsh campaign of 1165. When Richard deserted his father in 1189 he took a large part of his father's mercenary force with him and this, more than anything else, led to the King's defeat. The decisive action of this final campaign took place in June at LeMans. Richard, aided by the French king, set fire to the town, driving Henry northward. Many of Henry's mercenaries lost their lives at LeMans, leaving the English king defenseless. With his hired forces gone, Henry had no alternative but to sue for peace. But Henry died before the plan could be put into effect.

The accounts of these campaigns in Aquitaine supply us with the names of specific mercenary captains. One such leader was an apostate cleric, William of Cambresis, who played a large role in Richard's defense of his father's lands against the lords of La Marche, Angoulême, Limousin and Poitou. Another mercenary contingent was led by Lupatius who seems to have done most of his fighting in the Limousin. In 1182 the Limousin was also the scene of an invasion by a group of *coterels* led by Courbaran and Sancho of Saragnac. But the most famous mercenary captain of the period was Mercadier, a Brabantine in Richard's employ. Although his greatest services were rendered in the 1190's defending King Richard's continental lands against the French king, Philip Augustus, he is heard of as early as 1183 leading his followers through Perigord. Mercadier was to remain the leader of Richard's continental forces throughout his reign.

This brief survey of Henry's overseas wars brings into focus several points of institutional importance. In the first place, there was a step-by-step development in the type of mercenaries used. The early campaigns were fought with paid troops drawn almost exclusively from northern France—Brabantines and, occasionally, Flemings. Beginning fitfully with the Toulouse campaign in 1159 and more consistently after the Welsh war of 1165, mercenaries from Wales took their place alongside the continental recruits. For the later expeditions in southern France, Richard made use of paid troops from the local area, as is seen from his employment of Gascons against his brother Henry.

It is also likely that by the second half of his reign Henry was budgeting money for his mercenaries and was able to pay them from the normal annual revenues of the kingdom. This is suggested by the collection of only one scutage after 1172, and that one (1186–87) for an exceptional campaign to Ireland. Not only was room made for soldiers' salaries in the annual budget, but a new term appeared to designate these funds. The first use of the phrase *milites solidarii* is found in the Pipe Roll of 1162. From that year on the term was used with increasing frequency until by the end of the reign it had taken its place in the standard list of expressions found in the rolls.

There is every reason to believe that Henry's policy for the island was identical to the one he pursued on the Continent. Objecttions have been raised against this idea, as has been seen, by the nineteenth-century medieval historian, Bishop Stubbs. It was his contention, and that of most historians since his time, that in the absence of knight-service and mercenaries the defense of the island was left to a "national militia," a continuation of the Anglo-Saxon fyrd. Feudal lords were not used, they say, because of the distinct possibility that knight-service might prejudice the royal power, whereas the very name "mercenary" was so distasteful to the English people that "an attempt to support a standing army of such materials would have been a signal for rebellion." [4] There are several important points to be considered here before turning to the record. True, Henry did not depend on feudal fighters to defend the island, but not for the reason suggested by the bishop. The decay of martial spirit among the nobles and their preoccupation with Henry's burgeoning bureaucracy appear as more plausible motives. As for mercenaries, the suggestion that the English people would not have tolerated them is an anachronistic proposal put forth by an historian caught up in the nineteenth-century English democratic deluge into attributing similar attitudes to Englishmen seven centuries earlier. Although it is true that Henry was more conscious of the opinions of his subjects than many contemporary—and even succeeding—monarchs, it is inconceivable that he would permit such a vague climate of opinion to deter him from so obvious and necessary a military policy.

The theory that Henry relied upon a "national militia" to defend England rests on two shaky pieces of evidence. One is the Assize of Arms issued in 1181. The other is the island phase of the rebellion of 1173–74. Neither of these is strong enough to support the proposed role of the fyrd. While the Assize did provide in theory for the arming of all freemen there is no indication that it was put to use during Henry's reign. Some modern critics have noted that the Assize, rather than creating a non-feudal force, simply shifted the undertenants' allegiance from their lords to the king by placing these vassals under the sheriffs of the counties. They conclude that "neither the Assize of Arms nor later legislation, while imposing compulsory military equipment and training, created a conscript army or converted the local levies into an effective striking force." [5] This whole question as to whether or not an effective national militia existed at the time of Henry is part of a larger discussion concerning the survival of the Anglo-Saxon fyrd into Norman-Angevin times. Some recent scholarship is of the opinion that "the fyrd of Freeman and Stubbs and their followers is an imaginary institution, a wishful illusion." [6]

Our earlier description of the revolt of Henry's sons in 1173–74 passed over in silence the military action that took place in England. An analysis of the island campaigns during these two years shows that Henry relied upon his mercenaries during the decisive phase of operations against the rebels. During the first year of revolt there were three military encounters in England. Henry's forces were successful in all three, although probably without mercenaries, who had enough to keep them occupied on the Continent. In the first action, during July, the town and castle of Leicester were besieged by the royal forces under the command of Richard of Lucy and the Earl of Cornwall. The King's troops are referred to simply as the "army of England." After a three-week siege proved fruitless, Henry's allies burned the city but still failed to take the castle. In the following month William the Lion, King of Scotland, took advantage of Henry's preoccupation abroad to invade England. Richard of Lucy marched north and chased the king of the Scots to the safety of Berwick. The English followed him and created such havoc that William sued for peace. In this campaign also the English forces are unspecified by the reporters and probably were made up of a combination of feudal and local levies.

Richard was forced to halt the campaign short of total victory and accept the peace terms because of the sudden onset of the third major campaign of the year, the "Leicester War." Robert, Earl of Leicester, and chief opponent of the King on the island, landed in East Anglia in September at the head of a large body of Flemish mercenaries. He went immediately to Hugh Bigod's castle at Framlingham, and from there attempted to cross the island to his own shire of Leicester. He was intercepted and captured by a small English army near Bury St. Edmund. Again there is nothing to indicate the presence of mercenaries in the royal force. It probably contained the same mixture of feudal and local levies as in the two preceding engagements. The first year of the revolt in England ended on a successful note for Henry and showed that non-paid forces were adequate for the defense of the island against isolated and sporadic eruptions. The three campaigns had followed one another in succession, and at no time were the royal forces faced with an engagement on more than one front.

During the following year, however, these challenges coalesced and the local levies were unable to cope with the situation. At the request of Richard of Lucy, who was facing William the Lion in the north and Hugh Bigod in the east, Henry brought his mercenaries over from the Continent. He arrived in July and it took him but one month to dispose of the threat and bring the revolt to an end. The mercenaries defeated Hugh Bigod and were back on the Continent by August for the prosecution of the war there. Despite the shortness of their stay on the island, hired troops accounted for the rebels' defeat. They accomplished in one month what the "militia" had been unable to do in twelve.

Except for these two years of family revolt, England was at peace under Henry II. The key to this peace was a network of royal castles, which a contemporary referred to as "the bones of the kingdom." [7] The barons also had castles, of course, and from time to time they proved troublesome. However, they could pose a major threat only by joining to present a united front against Henry. This the King prevented by the strategic location of his strongholds. Royal castles, plus the general diminution of warlike ardor among the lords, neutralized the baronial castles causing them to lose their military significance before the end of the reign.[8] Therefore a study of the English defense posture during the second half of the twelfth century must deal primarily with royal fortifications and the people who garrisoned them. It is evident from the Pipe Rolls that the feudal service of castle guard had by then trod the same path toward commutation as had knight-service, and the English soldiers who manned the royal castles were paid for their duty.

The strategic location of Henry's castles reflects an appreciation on the part of the King of previous military threats to the island kingdom. His defense network polarized around four areas: the main waterways leading into the country; the coastline; the Welsh marches; and the Scottish frontier. Henry spent large sums of money improving his castles in these four vital regions, and an analysis of these expenditures shows a direct proportion between a particular threat and the defense appropriations for castle construction at any given time.[9] In the early part of his reign special attention was paid to those castles which faced the Welsh in the west. During and after the revolt of 1173–74 funds were diverted to royal fortifications in the east and north—the two regions threatened by the rebels. Coastal forts received constant attention since the possibility of invasion from any external quarter never disappeared.

The same was true of the English soldiers who guarded these fortifications. Until the waning of the Welsh threat in 1165 the royal castles in the marcher shires of Chester, Shropshire and Hereford received the lion's share of the money for mercenaries. The castles of Shropshire had the most hired garrisons. Entries appear almost annually of salaries paid to soldiers at Whittington, Shrawardine, Clun, Ruthin, and Oswestry. The four latter fortifications were held by William fitz Alan and his descendants, and the Pipe Roll entries illustrate that the King was not above sending mercenaries to bolster baronial castles in time of emergency. Further south, in Hereford, the kingdom's defense was strengthened by royal mercenaries in the castles of Skenfrith, Grosmont and White

Castle. Between 1165 and the revolt in 1173, Henry concentrated his mercenaries at Oswestry. Whether the other castles reverted to their peacetime role as administrative centers, or whether they were guarded by feudal service, we do not know. If, indeed, as seems probable, their defense was entrusted to knights, this would provide further proof that feudal service was adequate in times of relative calm, but that mercenaries were necessary to counter any major threat to the kingdom.

In 1173 and 1174 expenditures for castle mercenaries began to flow to the eastern and northern reaches of England. Many castles appear for the first time during these years as recipients of money for the payment of their garrisons. In the eastern counties, for example, the officers and men of the coastal strongholds of Hastings, Colchester, Oxford, Norwich, Bungay, Framlingham and Porchester were paid from royal revenues. All of these castles were in Henry's hands by 1174. Any rebel invasion from the Continent would have been met first by mercenaries stationed in these fortifications. A second line of defense was formed by those inland castles which protected the main waterways into the kingdom. These, too, were manned with hired soldiers during the rebellion. Henry's money, for example, supported the garrisons at Northampton, Salisbury, Windsor, Nottingham, Worcester, Hertford, Newcastle-under-Lyme and Warwick, to name a few. Finally, the royal accounts mention the presence of mercenaries in the northern castles of Prudhoe, Newcastle-on-Tyne, Bolsover, Peak, Cambridge, Wark-on-Tweed and Kenilworth, many of which were baronial rather than royal possessions. Since the war against the Scots was more "national" than civil, the presence of royal mercenaries in these castles is not surprising.

The payment of salaries to castle personnel reached a peak in 1173-74. After this period such payments virtually disappeared from the records. Coincidentally, building costs were recorded with more frequency.[10] The art of castle construction had reached, by the late twelfth century, a point of sophistication which allowed the monarch to dispense with large garrisons of men in peacetime. Under these circumstances the feudal service of castle guard was adequate for defense in normal situations. During wartime, however, such as in 1173 and 1174, Henry defended his kingdom with paid castle garrisons just as he relied upon mercenaries in the continental phase of the rebellion.

Although most of Henry's defense budget was spent in manning castles, some of it went to hire naval mercenaries. As with the land forces, expenditures for naval equipment and personnel increased greatly during times of threat. The rolls of the years 1172 through 1174 are dotted with references to salaries for ship captains and sailors for their part in defending the island. In 1173 a large armada of ships was gathered from each of the English maritime counties and dispatched to the island of Sandwich to defend against invasion. The King's money bought soldiers for the sea as well as for the land, on the island as well as abroad, and for defense as well as for offense.

In summary, then, Henry Plantagenet expanded the areas from which mercenaries were recruited. For his continental campaigns he depended during the early years almost exclusively upon mercenaries from northern France. These were joined after 1165 by Welsh mercenaries. The monarch's reliance on paid soldiers stemmed from a reluctance to interfere with the peaceful administrative and judicial pursuits of his nobility. At home Henry entrusted his island to well-situated and well-built castles which he filled during times of threat with paid troops. Mercenaries, therefore, were the backbone of Henry's army and can to no small degree be credited with helping the monarch to strengthen his own position and that of his successors.

The annual revenues of the kingdom during the early years of Henry's reign were meager compared to those of his grandfather, Henry I. The second Henry overcame this by perfecting the institution of scutage, the returns of which were used to pay his mercenaries. Of his seven scutage collections, all but the last were made during the first half of the reign.[11] After 1172 Henry was able to pay his hired soldiers from the normal revenues. Mercenaries had by then become recognized as a regular expenditure in the annual budget.

CHAPTER VI

Conclusion

MERCENARIES, both foreign and native, comprised an essential part of medieval English armies and made substantial contributions to the military successes of the Anglo-Norman and the first of the Angevin rulers. William the Conqueror had a large number in his invading host and continued to use them to pacify the island and to neutralize the threats to his rule from his nobles. William II was seriously challenged by his brother Robert on two occasions and both revolts were defeated largely with hired troops. He also used mercenaries to extend the boundaries of his continental lands. Henry I's reign was marked by two military turning points—in England in 1102 and on the Continent four years later. In each case mercenaries played an important role in the king's success.

Stephen of Blois remained on the English throne from 1135 to 1154 despite a civil war. Hired soldiers contributed to his success. During his reign mercenaries were organized and placed under a permanent leader, William of Ypres. They were mostly Flemings and appeared prominently in most major military engagements of the reign. The year 1141 was a watershed in Stephen's fortunes. The leader of the rebel forces, Robert of Gloucester, was captured at Winchester thereby offsetting the many advantages that Robert had accrued up till then. Significantly he was captured by Stephen's Flemings under William of Ypres.

Reliance on mercenaries continued under Henry II who leaned heavily upon them for his campaigns on the Continent, in Wales, in Ireland, and in England. Further, Henry entrusted the defense of England itself to hired garrisons in royal castles. The presence of mercenaries in important roles at the key battles of each of these reigns illustrates their significance in English medieval military and institutional history.

This willingness of English monarchs to include mercenaries among their fighting forces indicates that the twelfth century was institutionally fluid. These rulers were relatively unfettered by past tradition in their choice of institutions and were free to experiment with various military forms. Mercenary use developed essentially from two sets of conditions: those that forced rulers to experiment with hired forces, and those that provided them with sufficient freedom to conduct such experiments.

The Conqueror was forced to hire soldiers primarily because he could not depend on the loyalty of his Normans. This was true both before and after he came to England. As Duke of Normandy he experienced four major revolts; and as King of England, two. Before his death half of the leading barons who supported his invasion had revolted against him. Under the circumstances he had nowhere else to turn but to mercenaries. He was able to hire fighters as a result of his sound financial position. Before 1066 William, alone among continental rulers, managed to keep firmly within his grasp the hard-cash revenues of his duchy. His centralization of the political and financial machinery in England after the Conquest placed him in a favorable position to purchase warriors. The addition of confiscated sources of revenue greatly increased this capability.

These conditions became even more pronounced during the reign of the Conqueror's namesake son. Like his father, William II had to guard constantly against Norman disloyalty and faced major rebellions on three occasions. Mercenaries were used to quiet each of them. But Rufus was less successful than his father in keeping tight the reigns of government and had to employ extraordinary fund-raising measures to support his armies. In this way scutage got its start.

This same disloyalty plagued Henry I during the early years of his reign. Like his father and brother before him, it was the rebellious nature of Robert Curthose that forced the monarch to rely heavily upon soldiers whose loyalty could be bought and who on that account were more trustworthy than the feudal nobility. That disloyalty was behind Henry's employment of mercenaries is suggested by the existence of a direct ratio between the degree of revolt and the hiring of soldiers. After the rebellion subsided in England in 1102, mercenary use on the island came to an end, although it continued on the Continent. Henry was able to hire mercenaries as a result of his financial administration which was so well organized that at the end of his reign it brought in over £66,000 annually to the Crown. The institution of scutage was further developed, as was the system of accounting for shire revenues. All in all it appears that Henry was in an excellent financial position to use mercenaries. Like his predecessors disloyalty forced him to hire soldiers and his wealth permitted him to do so.

During the civil war Stephen used mercenaries to compensate for the loss of feudal support. His alienation of much of the Church at the beginning of the war made it easier for him to hire soldiers. His wealth made him independent and capable of using non-feudal military forces. This wealth he derived from his own widespread domain, Henry I's treasury, and confiscated Church lands.

The driving force behind Henry II's use of mercenaries was not disloyalty nor disunity but the disinterest of his nobles in military affairs. The long period of peace at home, coupled with the King's emphasis on the development of administrative institutions, diverted the attention and energies of his feudal tenants-in-chief from martial to peaceful pursuits. In turn, the financial sophistication which resulted gave Henry more than enough money with which to hire soldiers. His strong control of the Exchequer and his extension of the system of scutage provided him with the funds and freedom to recruit an army.

Each English ruler between 1066 and 1189 was faced, therefore, with conditions which on the one hand forced him to experiment with mercenaries, and on the other provided him with the economic viability to carry out such a policy. There is discernible in the course of these experiments a progressive development of the mercenary policy from the sporadic use of hired troops in the beginning to a regular dependence on them at the end of the period. Furthermore, the geographical areas which supplied the military manpower expanded as the period progressed. Prior to Henry II

mercenaries came almost exclusively from northern France, especially from Flanders and Brittany. Henry's contacts with Wales
and his addition of southern France to the empire opened these
areas as recruiting grounds. In addition, Henry paid native Englishmen to help in the defense of their homeland. This progression is
a further instance of institutional flexibility in the twelfth century.

While disloyalty, disunity and disinterest led on the one hand,
to a mercenary policy, on the other it prevented the operation of
an effective system of knight-service. Feudal military service was
predicated upon the loyal attachment of vassal to lord and upon
the actual interest and ability of both to perform in a martial
capacity. The absence of this attachment, interest, and, at times,
ability, was striking. Knight-service, therefore, could hardly have
formed, in practice, the basis for an army as it is purported to
have done in theory. Records of enfeoffment and legal treatises concerning feudal military service present us only with an ideal. For
the most part the reality was quite different. The fact that lip-
service was paid to the theory throughout the period suggests that
the system of knight-service was a financial arrangement designed
to produce not warriors but the money with which to hire them.

In the larger picture, the prevalence of mercenaries in the
twelfth century provides food for thought concerning the "newness" of the new monarchies and the use of mercenaries in the
fifteenth and sixteenth centuries. Some have suggested that many
of the vehicles used by the English and French rulers of these
centuries to strengthen their royal position were actually revivals
or even continuations of earlier, medieval institutions. There is
abundant evidence to suggest that the institution of mercenaries
falls into this category. The importance of mercenaries in sixteenth-
century Italy is well known through the writings of Machiavelli.
Since he was the first writer in modern times to treat mercenaries
in an organized way, the impression is gained that the hiring of
soldiers was in his time a new phenomenon or, at least, a revival of
earlier Roman practice. In fact, it arrived in Italy from the north
where it had enjoyed a continuous existence since the Middle Ages.
The main obstacle to an appreciation of this fact has been a one-
sided interpretation of medieval records. It seems much closer to

the facts to view mercenaries as another inheritance passed on from the medieval period to the Renaissance. Had Machiavelli lived in twelfth-century England he could have written no less voluminously about contemporary mercenaries than he did in sixteenth-century Florence.

MILITARY CAMPAIGNS AND SIEGES
(1066-1189)

THE following list contains only those campaigns of the English kings which lasted longer than the annual term of feudal military service. Sieges are included as illustrative of the important role they played in medieval warfare. This information has been compiled principally from contemporary narrative sources and for that reason the dates and durations are approximate but of sufficient accuracy for the purposes of this table.

YEAR	CAMPAIGN	SIEGES	DATES	DURATION (in months)
WILLIAM I				
1066	Norman conquest		Aug.–Dec.	4
1069–70	Yorkshire		Sep.–Jan.	4
1070	Western England		Jan.–Apr.	3
1075	Against Roger of Hereford and Ralph of Norfolk	Hereford Norwich		3
WILLIAM II				
1088	Baronial revolt in eastern England	Pevensey Rochester		2
1091	Invasion of the Scots		Sep.–Dec.	3
1095	Baronial revolt	Newcastle Tynemouth Bamborough		5
HENRY I				
1102	Revolt of Robert of Bellême	Arundel Tickhill Bridgnorth Shrewsbury		6

YEAR	CAMPAIGN	SIEGES	DATES	DURATION (in months)
1118	On the Continent	Laigle Alençon	Jul.–Dec.	5
1119	On the Continent	Evreux	Jun.–Oct.	4
1123–24	On the Continent		Oct.–Dec.	2

STEPHEN

1136	Scots invasion		Feb.–Mar.	1
	Revolt of Hugh Bigod		Apr.	1
	Revolt of Robert of Bampton		Jun.	1
	Revolt of Baldwin		Jun.–Sep.	3
			TOTAL FOR 1136	6
1137	Against Geoffrey of Anjou		Mar.–Nov.	8
1137–8	Revolt of Miles of Beauchamp	Bedford	Dec.–Jan.	1½
1138	Northallerton		Feb.	½
	Revolt of Geoffrey Talbot	Hereford Woebley	Apr.–Jun.	2
	Against the Empress	Castle Carey Harptree Shrewsbury		
		Dover	Jun.–Sep.	3
			TOTAL FOR 1138	5½
1139	Against Robert of Gloucester	Dunster Corfe Marlborough Arundel Wallingford Cerney Malmesbury Trowbridge	Aug.–Dec.	4
1140–41	Against the Empress	Lincoln	Dec.–Feb.	2
1141	Against the Empress	Winchester	Jun.–Aug.	2
1142	Against the Empress	Wareham Cirencester Bampton Radcot Oxford	Jun.–Dec.	6

YEAR	CAMPAIGN	SIEGES	DATES	DURATION (in months)
1144	Against Geoffrey of Mandeville		Apr.–Sep.	5
1147	Against Gilbert fitz Richard of Clare	Pevensey		"a long time"
1149	Eustace's campaign against Henry of Anjou		Summer– Dec.	6
1152	Against the Empress	Wallingford Worcester Newbury		12
1153	Against Henry of Anjou	Ipswich	Jan.–Nov.	10

HENRY II

YEAR	CAMPAIGN	SIEGES	DATES	DURATION (in months)
1156	Against Geoffrey	Chinon Mirabeau	Feb.–May	3
		Limoges and Thouars	Oct.	1
1159	Toulouse	Toulouse	Jun.–Sep.	3
1160	On the Continent	Chatillon	May–Aug.	3
1165	Wales		May–Aug.	3
1166	Maine and Brittany	Alençon Fougères	Mar.–Jul.	4
1167	Auvergne, Normandy and Brittany	Chaumont	Apr.–Sep.	5
1168	Poitou, Brittany and Normandy	Lusignan	May–Dec.	7
1169	Poitou and Gascony		Mar., Jun.– Aug.	3
1171–72	Ireland		Sep.–Aug.	11
1173	On the Continent		Jun.–Nov.	5
1174	On the Continent and in England	Huntingdon	Apr.–Sep.	5
1183	On the Continent	Limoges	Jan.–Jun.	5
1188	On the Continent		Jul.–Dec.	5
1189	On the Continent		Jan.–Jul.	6

THE FRAGMENTATION OF KNIGHTS' FEES
(1135–1166)

IT has long been recognized that the practice of granting fiefs in return for the service of less than a full knight dates back at least as far as the time of Henry I. Instances have been noted by A. L. Poole and F. M. Stenton,[1] although neither author has drawn the conclusion that, since such responsibilities could only have been discharged by a money payment, the fragmentation of fees was incompatible with feudalism as defined by John H. Round. Although it is not the aim of the present study to discuss this point directly, the conclusion derived from fragmentation of fees combines with that resulting from a demonstration of the importance of mercenaries to modify seriously the theory of the existence of a militarily effective system of knight-service in the twelfth century.

The following table, derived from the *Cartae Baronum* of 1166,[2] clearly illustrates that

> There are more cases than is always realized in which a baron will return among his fees of the old enfeoffment tenancies carrying a very small part of a knight's service: a fifth, a tenth, or even a twentieth.[3]

[1] A. L. Poole, *Obligations of Society in the Twelfth and Thirteenth Centuries* (Oxford: Clarendon Press, 1946), p. 46; F. M. Stenton, *The First Century of English Feudalism, 1066–1166* (2d. ed. rev.; Oxford: Clarendon Press, 1961), pp. 187–90.

[2] *Red Book of the Exchequer*, ed. Hubert Hall (London: H. M. Stationery Office, 1896), pp. 186–445.

[3] Stenton, *op. cit.*, p. 188.

COUNTY OR CITY	TOTAL NUMBER OF TENANCIES LISTED	TENANCIES HELD FOR ONE-HALF KNIGHT'S FEE [1]	TENANCIES HELD FOR LESS THAN ONE-HALF KNIGHT'S FEE
Bedfordshire	76	21	19
Berkshire	74	18	4
Buckinghamshire	73	15	2
Cambridgeshire	87	8	23
Cornwall	20		1
Derbyshire	37	6	
Devonshire	219	55	36
Dorsetshire	93	12	22
Essex	181	44	10
Gloucestershire	134	24	14
Herefordshire	100	12	8
Hertfordshire	29	11	5
Huntingdonshire	24	8	6
Kent	103	36	10
Lancaster	1		
Leicestershire	10	2	
Lincolnshire	195	32	33
London	37	12	17
Middlesex	17	3	2
Norfolk	149	37	22
Northamptonshire	44	18	8
Northumberland	25	2	4
Nottinghamshire	42	8	2
Oxfordshire	18		2
Shropshire	67	4	
Somerset	183	36	20
Southampton	71	4	
Staffordshire	88	30	26
Suffolk	115	37	13
Surrey	4		2
Sussex	66	7	2
Warwickshire	47	6	6
Wiltshire	100	23	4
Worcestershire	39	15	2
Yorkshire	296	55	54
TOTAL	2864	601	379

[1] Enfeoffments for increments of one-half a knight's fee (½, 1½, 2½, etc.) are included in this column and are listed separately from smaller fragments since this service could possibly be discharged by sending a sergeant to the royal array. Even should these not be counted as "fragmented" for our purposes, the total of enfeoffments for less than one-half a knight's fee remains impressive.

APPENDIX C

VALUE IN POUNDS OF THE LAND HELD BY THE TEN LEADING COMPANIONS OF WILLIAM THE CONQUEROR

(Domesday Book—1086)

	Wm. fitz Osbern[1] 1075, 1078	Odo of Bayeux 1082, 1088	Roger of Montgomery 1078, 1088, 1095, 1102, 1106	Robert of Mortain 1088, 1102	Hugh of Avranches	Eustace of Boulogne 1067, 1088, 1101	Geoffrey of Mandeville	Geoffrey of Coutances 1088, 1095	William of Warrenne 1101	Ralph the Staller 1075
Bedfordshire						21		47	8	
Berkshire	41			3	29		59	5		
Buckinghamshire		169		108	29			92	13	
Cambridgeshire			30	10		37	63		51	
Cheshire					206					
Cornwall				406						
Derbyshire					3					

Land forfeited—1075[1]: Not included in Domesday

Devonshire	6		139				142	118
Dorsetshire			181	3			8	2
Essex				44	484	304	20	6
Gloucestershire		3	2	50				
Hampshire	71	114	8	3	60	160		
Hertfordshire					76			
Huntingdonshire			55	9	15			
Kent	1588				80			
Leicestershire		25	16	42				
Lincolnshire	143		8	178				
Middlesex							1	10
Norfolk	99		127	88	21	112		12
Northamptonshire	14		7	35		27	100	
Nottinghamshire	10		6	4				
Oxfordshire	406			70		20		
Shropshire	11				2			15
Somerset		939	336	10	31		340	
Staffordshire		91		94				
Suffolk	180	22	51		22	22		
Surrey			9		49	33		
Sussex		838	338	2				22
Warwickshire	14	33		16				
Wiltshire	21	22	11			31	2	
Worcestershire	6						25	
Yorkshire		21	83	11				502
TOTAL:	2779	2138	1904	926	898	831	782	759

[1] Italicized date indicates the year of a rebellion by an original companion of the Conqueror; where the date is not italicized the reference is to a rebellion by a descendant.

SCUTAGE TOTALS
FOR THE REIGN OF HENRY II [1]
(1154–1189)

PIPE ROLL YEAR	TOTAL COLLECTED [2]		
	£	s.	d.
1155–56	2229	17	11
1158–59	7708	18	11
1160–61	2461	11	4
1161–62	1642	5	4
1164–65	2076	4	0
1171–72	2137	0	5
1186–87	1978	13	2

[1] From the Pipe Rolls 2, 5, 7, 8, 11, 18, and 33 Henry II.
[2] Includes *dona* and *auxilia* where these sums are not specifically earmarked.

ANNUAL EXPENDITURES FOR CASTLE SOLDIERS AND CASTLE CONSTRUCTION (1158–1189)

THE sums listed include only those specifically earmarked for salaries. Wages paid to soldiers for duties other than serving in a castle, such as for a Welsh or Norman expedition, for bearing a summons or guarding the treasure, are not included. The salaries of *milites* and *servientes* are lumped together.

The list is not restricted to royal castles but includes those baronial fortifications upon which royal money was spent for defense. Castles whose garrisons received a combined total of £20 or more are listed separately in the third column. This gives an indication of the geographical areas of concentration.

PIPE ROLLS	TOTAL SALARIES			SALARIES BY CASTLE				BUILDING COSTS		
	£	s.	d.		£	s.	d.	£	s.	d.
1158–59	8	7	3					291	12	2½
1159–60	248	5		Walton	126			468	10	9
				Chester	35	5	10			
1160–61	256	0	8	Walton	115	11	8	258	4	2
				Dover	25		22			
1161–62	147	5	1	Kent	56	1	4	160	15	1
				Pevensey	20	3	4			
1162–63	54	4	8					83	11	8
1163–64	151	5	5	Dover	28	6	8	129	1	4½
				Walton	24	0	20			

PIPE ROLLS	TOTAL SALARIES			SALARIES BY CASTLE				BUILDING COSTS		
	£	s.	d.		£	s.	d.	£	s.	d.
1164–65	187	5	4	Shrawardine	75	18	7	24	8	9
				Oswestry	62	7	5			
				Dover	25					
1165–66	158	5	4	Abergavenny	65	2	2	746	9	11
				Shrawardine	62		16			
				Chirck	31		11			
1166–67	160	16	8	Oswestry	160	16	8	483	13	1
1167–68	225	12	10	Windsor	84	2		576	11	4
				Oswestry	33	16	8			
				Walton	25		10			
1168–69	83	16	10	Oswestry	31	8	4	422	8	6
1169–70	69	19	2	Oswestry	60	16	8	481	7	1
				(for 2 yrs.)						
1670–71	39	10	10	Oswestry	30	8	4	1137	18	7
1171–72	48	1	18	Oswestry	30	8	4	1337	9	0
1172–73	893	18	10	Orford	159	9	1	2155	16	0
				Northampton	152	8	4			
				Nottingham, Bolsover, Peak	135					
				Berkhamstead	65	3	4			
				Salisbury	63	1				
				Norwich	44	13	4			
				Hastings	43	14	3			
				Lincoln	40					
				Stafford	33	5				
				Oswestry	30	8	4			
				Colchester	29	15				
				Newcastle-On-Tyne	20					
				Prudhoe	20					
1173–74	1252			Kenilworth	180	41	8	754	12	11
				Northampton	171					
				Lincoln	158					
				Nottingham, Bolsover, Peak	138	4	8			
				Porchester	88					
				Salisbury	55	13	8			

PIPE ROLLS	TOTAL SALARIES			SALARIES BY CASTLE				BUILDING COSTS		
	£	s.	d.		£	s.	d.	£	s.	d.
1173–74				Oswestry	48	13	4			
				Newcastle-under-Lyme	47	9	2			
				Norwich	46	4	4			
				Canterbury	43					
				Warwick	42	10				
				Walton	42	6	8			
				Wark	41					
				Worcester	26	13	4			
				Hastings	26					
				Orford	20					
1174–75	5315	130	83	Yorkshire	1228	16	10[1]	616	19	1
				Lancaster	1076	2	2[1]			
				Worcester	63	6	8			
				Oswestry	37	10				
				Shrewsbury, Bridgnorth	28	13	11			
1176–77	35	14	3					537	12	3
1177–78	—	—	—					513	3	2
1178–79	—	—	—					410	14	8
1179–80	—	—	—					658	14	9
1180–81	—	—	—					462	9	9
1181–82	—	—	—					1487	2	8
1182–83	—	—	—					917	2	5
1183–84	—	—	—					978	16	6
1184–85	440	3	3	Neath, Newburgh, Cardiff, Newcastle	277	8	10	1844	4	11½
				Kenfig	22	19	4			
1185–86	—	—	—					1462	0	11½
1186–87	—	—	—					978	9	10
1187–88	—	—	—					307	3	9
1188–89	—	—	—					168	4	3

[1] Denotes money spent for soldiers to defend against the Scots, even though specific castles are not mentioned.

Notes

These notes represent but a fifteenth part of the notes of the original manuscript. The author invites correspondence concerning the documentation of any portion of this work.

CHAPTER 1

1. Round's thesis is found in his essay "The Introduction of Knight Service into England," which was reprinted from the *English Historical Review* in his *Feudal England*, 1909, pp. 225–314.

2. By, among others, C. Warren Hollister, "The Norman Conquest and the Genesis of English Feudalism," *American Historical Review*, LXVI (April 1961), pp. 653–54.

3. C.W.C. Oman, *The Art of War in the Middle Ages*, ed. John Beeler, 1953, p. 57.

4. See Appendix A.

5. J. O. Prestwich, "War and Finance in the Anglo-Norman State," *Transactions of the Royal Historical Society*, 5th series, IV (1954), pp. 42–3.

CHAPTER 2

1. *Gesta Stephani*, trans. K. R. Potter, 1955, p. 102.

2. Austin Lane Poole, *From Domesday Book to Magna Carta, 1087–1215*, 1951, p. 140.

3. C. Warren Hollister, "The Annual Term of Military Service in Medieval England," *Mediaevalia et Humanistica*, XIII, p. 45.

4. See Appendix A.

5. See Appendix B.

6. Norman F. Cantor, *The Medieval World 300–1300*, 1963, p. 66.

CHAPTER 3

1. David C. Douglas, *William the Conqueror*, 1964, p. 41.

2. G. Littleton, *History of the Life of King Henry II*, 1767, I, 523.

3. Henry of Huntingdon, *Historiae Anglorum*, ed. Arnold, 1879, p. 199.

4. See Appendix C.

5. Orderic Vitalis, *Historiae Ecclesiasticae*, ed. Prevost 1838–55, II, 379.

6. F. M. Stenton, *The First Century of English Feudalism, 1066–1166*, 2nd ed. 1961, p. 151.

7. William of Malmesbury, *De Gestis Regum Anglorum*, ed. Stubbs 1887–89, II, 299.

8. Florence of Worcester, *Chronicon ex Chronicis*, 1592, p. 440.

9. William of Malmesbury, *op. cit.*, II, 379.

CHAPTER 4

1. William of Malmesbury, *Historia Novella*, trans. K. R. Potter, 1955, p. 57.

2. *Gesta Stephani*, trans. K. R. Potter, 1955, p. 116.

3. *Ibid.*, p. 146.

4. *Ibid.*, p. 53.

5. *Ibid.*

6. *Ibid.*, p. 79.

7. *Ibid.*, pp. 102–103.

CHAPTER 5

1. William Stubbs, *The Constitutional History of England*, 1897, I, 630.

2. See Appendix D.

3. Robert of Torigni, *Chronicle*, in *Chronicles of the Reigns of Stephen, Henry II and Richard I*, ed. R. Howlett, 1889, p. 202.

4. Benedict of Peterborough, *Chronicle of the Reigns of Henry II and Richard I*, ed. William Stubbs, 1867, p. civ.

5. H. G. Richardson and G. O. Sayles, *The Governance of Mediaeval England from the Conquest to Magna Carta*, 1963, p. 76.

6. *Ibid.*, p. 55.

7. William of Newburgh, *Historia Rerum Anglicarum*, 1884, I, 331.

8. F. M. Stenton, *The First Century of English Feudalism, 1066–1166*, 2nd ed., 1961, p. 194.

9. See Appendix E.

10. See Appendix E.

11. See Appendix D.

BIBLIOGRAPHY

THIS list incorporates only those works which have been of the most direct value in the preparation of the present study. The critical comments appended to the secondary works are made solely from the viewpoint of their contribution, be it positive or negative, to the question of the importance of mercenaries.

PRIMARY MATERIALS

Aelred of Rievaulx. *Relatio de Standardo* in *Chronicles of the Reigns of Stephen, Henry II and Richard I*. ed. R. Howlett. (Rolls Series). London: Longman and Co., 1886.
Amplissima Collectio Sacrorum Conciliorum. ed. J. D. Mansi. Leipzig: F. M. Guidel, 1903.
Anglo-Saxon Chronicle. ed. B. Thorpe. (Rolls Series). London: Longman, Green, Longman and Roberts, 1861.
Benedict of Peterborough. *Chronicle of the Reigns of Henry II and Richard I.* ed. William Stubbs. (Rolls Series). 2 vols. London: Longman, Green, Reader and Dyer, 1867.
Domesday Book. 2 vols. London: 1783.
Florence of Worcester. *Chronicon ex Chronicis.* ed. William Howard. London: Thomas Dawson, 1592.
Foedera, Conventiones, Litterae et Cujuscunque Generis Acta Publica. ed. T. Rymer. 20 vols. London: Record Commission, 1816–69.
Geoffrey of Vigeois. *Chronicle* in *Recueil des historiens de Gaul et de la France.* 23 vols. Paris: 1737–1876. X, 267; XI, 288–89; XII, 421–50; XVIII, 211–23.
Gervase of Canterbury. *Chronicle.* ed. William Stubbs. (Rolls Series.) 2 vols. London: Longman and Co., 1879.
Gesta Stephani Regis Anglorum in *Chronicles of the Reigns of Stephen, Henry II and Richard I.* ed. R. Howlett. (Rolls Series) 4 vols. London: Longman and Co., 1886.
Gesta Stephani. ed. K. R. Potter. London: Thomas Nelson and Sons Ltd., 1955.

Henry of Huntingdon. *The History of the English.* ed. T. Arnold. (Rolls Series). London: Longman and Co., 1879.

Jordan Fantosme. *Chronicle* in *Chronicles of the Reigns of Stephen, Henry II and Richard I.* ed. R. Howlett. (Rolls Series) 4 vols. London: Longman and Co., 1886.

Lambert of Hersfeld. *Annales.* ed. Holder-Egger. Hanover: 1894.

Magni Rotuli Scaccari Normanniae sub Regibus Angliae. ed. Thomas Stapleton. 2 vols. London: J. B. Nichols, 1840–44.

Magnum Rotulum Scaccarii de Anno Tricesimo—Primo Regni Henrici Primi. ed. Joseph Hunter. London: Record Commission, 1833.

Magnus Rotulus Pipae, 1155–58. ed. Joseph Hunter. London: Record Commission, 1844.

The Murder of Charles the Good. trans. James Bruce Ross. New York: Columbia University Press, 1960.

Opera Lanfranci. ed. J. A. Giles. 2 vols. Oxford: Parker and Sons, 1844.

Orderici Vitalis Historiae Ecclesiasticae. ed. A. le Prevost. 5 vols. Paris: Renouard and Assoc., 1838–55.

Pipe Rolls, 5 Henry II to 1 Richard I. London: Pipe Roll Society, 1884–1919.

Ralph de Diceto. *Opera Historica.* ed. William Stubbs. (Rolls Series) 2 vols. London: H. M. Stationery Office, 1876.

Recueil des Chroniques de Flandre. ed. J. J. DeSmet. 4 vols. Brussels: M. Hayez, 1837–65.

Recueil des historiens des Gaules et de la France. 23 vols. Paris: 1737–1876.

Red Book of the Exchequer. ed. Hubert Hall. 3 vols. London: H. M. Stationery Office, 1896.

Regesta Regum Anglo-Normannorum 1066–1154. eds. H. W. C. Davis, Johnson and Cronne. 2 vols. Oxford: Clarendon Press, 1913.

Richard of Hexham. *De Gestis Regis Stephani* in *Chronicles of the Reigns of Stephen, Henry II and Richard I.* ed. R. Howlett. (Rolls Series.) 4 vols. London: Longman and Co., 1886.

Rigord. *Oeuvres de Rigord et de Guillaume le Breton, historiens de Philippe Auguste.* ed. M. Francois Delaborde. (Societé de l'histoire de France.) 2 vols. Paris: 1882–85.

Robert de Torigni. *Chronicle* in *Chronicles of the Reigns of Stephen, Henry II and Richard I.* ed. R. Howlett. (Rolls Series.) 4 vols. London: H. M. Stationery Office, 1889.

Roger of Hoveden. *Chronicle.* ed. Wm. Stubbs. (Rolls Series.) 4 vols. London: Longman and Co., 1868–71.

Simeon of Durham. *Historia Regum Simeonis Monachii.* ed. Wm. Stubbs. (Rolls Series.) London: Longman and Co., 1882–85.

Stephen of Rouen. *Draco Normannicus* in *Chronicles of the Reigns of Stephen, Henry II and Richard I.* ed. R. Howlett. (Rolls. Series.) 4 vols. London: Longman and Co., 1885.

Wace. *Roman de Rou et des ducs de Normandie.* ed. Hugo Andresen. 2 vols. Heilbronn: F. Vieweg, 1877–79.
William of Jumieges. *Gesta Normannorum Ducum.* ed. J. Marx. Paris: Auguste Picard, 1914.
William of Malmesbury. *Gesta Regum.* ed. Wm. Stubbs. (Rolls Series.) 2 vols. London: H. M. Stationery Office, 1887–89.
———. *Historia Novella.* trans. K. R. Potter. London: Thomas Nelson and Sons, 1955.
William of Newburgh. *Historia Rerum Anglicarum* in *Chronicles of the Reigns of Stephen, Henry II and Richard I.* ed. R. Howlett. (Rolls Series.) 4 vols. London: Longman and Co., 1884.
William of Poitiers. *Gesta Gullielmi ducis Normannorum et Regis Anglorum.* ed. Raymond Foreville. (Les classiques de l'histoire de France au moyen âge.) Paris: 1952.

SECONDARY WORKS

Barrow, G.W.S. *Feudal Britain: The Completion of the Medieval Kingdoms, 1066–1314.* London: Edward Arnold Ltd., 1956.
A useful survey of a long historical period which confines itself strictly to political developments.
Barlow, Frank. *The Feudal Kingdom of England, 1042–1216.* London: Longmans, Green & Co., 1955.
As the dates suggest, this work stresses the continuity of English institutional development before and after 1066.
———. *William I and the Norman Conquest.* London: English Universities Press, 1965.
Through his appreciation of the value of mercenaries to the Conqueror Barlow joins the revisionist school of medieval military institutions.
Beeler, John. *Warfare in England 1066–1189.* Ithaca: Cornell University Press, 1966.
One of the few books that attempts a full scale combination of military and institutional history. The military wins out.
———. "The Composition of Anglo-Norman Armies," *Speculum,* XL (1965), pp. 398–414.
The author acknowledges the frequent presence of mercenaries but continues to consider the knight as the most important element in the military establishment.
Boussard, Jacques. *Le gouvernment d'Henri II Plantegenêt.* Paris: Librairie D'Argences, 1956.
A comprehensive volume which treats, in turn, the geographical,

social, institutional and political milieu of the Angevin Empire under its founder. Recognizes the role of mercenaries.

————. "Les mercenaires au XII siècle. Henri II Plantegenêt et les origines de l'armée de métier," *Bibliothèque de l'Ecole des Chartes.* CVI (1947), pp. 189–224.
One of the earliest treatments of Henry II as an employer of mercenaries.

Brown, R. Allen. "Royal Castle-Building in England, 1154–1216," *English Historical Review,* LXX (1955), pp. 353–398, and "A List of Castles, 1154–1216," *English Historical Review,* LXXIV (1959), pp. 249–280.
Both articles contain valuable tabular information on English castles in Angevin times.

Chew, Helena M. *The English Ecclesiastical Tenants-in-Chief and Knight-Service.* Oxford: University Press, 1932.
Round's thesis of knight-service is supported by evidence from Church fiefs.

Coulborn, Rushton (ed.). *Feudalism in History.* Princeton: University Press, 1956.
A partially successful attempt to discover the existence of "feudalism" in eight different societies throughout history. Professor Strayer's chapter on western Europe is the only one of direct import to the present study.

Davis, H.W.C. *England Under the Normans and Angevins.* London: Methuen and Co., 1949.
A standard, detailed narrative of the period, important for the background it provides for the problem of paid service.

Davis, R.H.C. *King Stephen.* Berkeley: University of California Press, 1967.
This work appeared too late for consideration in this monograph. Davis argues against the common opinion that disloyalty was widespread under Stephen.

Dept, Gaston. "Les marchands Flamandes et le roi d'Angleterre," *Revue de Nord,* XII (1926), pp. 302–24.
Contains insights into the relations between England and the Flemings who often served as mercenaries.

Douglas, David C. *William the Conqueror: The Norman Impact upon England.* Berkeley: University of California Press, 1964.
Attributes William's successful conquest of England to his outstanding ability to set his pre-Conquest Norman house in order by taming and harnessing the energies of the secular and ecclesiastical aristocrats and using them to conquer and rule England. Mercenaries occupy a minute niche in this scheme.

Eyton, Robert W. *Court, Household and Itinerary of King Henry II.* London: Taylor, 1878.
An indispensable Baedeker for retracing the footsteps of the first Angevin monarch of England.

Freeman, Edward A. *History of the Norman Conquest of England*. 6 vols. Oxford: Clarendon Press, 1870–79.
Round's whipping boy in the development of his cataclysmic theory of the Norman Conquest. Useful as an illustration of pre-Roundian attitudes toward the Conquest.

George, Robert H. "The Contribution of Flanders to the Conquest of England," *Revue Belge de Philologie et d'Histoire*, V (1926), pp. 81–99.
Some added details on the Flemings that accompanied William to England.

Geraud, H. "Les routiers au XII siècle," *Bibliothèque de l'Ecole des Chartes*, II (1841), pp. 123–47.
Background on some of the displaced persons available on the Continent as mercenaries during the twelfth century.

Haskins, Charles H. *Norman Institutions*. Cambridge: Harvard University Press, 1918. (Reprint: New York; Frederick Ungar, 1960).
Supports the Round interpretation by pointing to similarities between knight-service in pre-Conquest Normandy and post-Conquest England.

Hollister, C. Warren. *Anglo-Saxon Military Institutions on the Eve of the Norman Conquest*. Oxford: Clarendon Press, 1962.
A major revision of Round's knight-service thesis which emphasizes neither knights nor mercenaries but the elite militia, the select fyrd.

———. *The Military Organization of Medieval England*. Oxford: Clarendon Press, 1965.
The fyrd, stressed in the earlier volume, remains an important alternative to knight-service after 1066. In this volume, however, mercenaries take their place alongside—or rather, to the left and a few paces behind —the militia.

———. "The Annual Term of Military Service in Medieval England," *Mediaevalia et Humanistica*, XIII, pp. 40–47.
Important for the study of mercenaries by showing that the annual term of knight-service decreased from sixty to forty days around the middle of the twelfth century.

Lot, Ferdinand. *L'art militaire et les armées au moyen âge*. 2 vols. Paris: Payot, 1946.
A primer for medieval military institutional developments, especially on the Continent.

———. et Fawtier, Robert (eds.). *Histoire des institutions Françaises au moyen âge*. 3 vols. (to date). Paris: Presses Universitaires de France, 1957–62.
A series of uneven essays by a multitude of authors synthesizing work done on French seigneurial, royal and ecclesiastical institutions. Particularly useful here for its treatment of the early "French" states.

Lyon, Bryce D. *From Fief to Indenture*. Cambridge: Harvard University Press, 1957.

A milestone publication which introduced the fief-rente, or money fief, into discussions of medieval institutions. It has remained there ever since.

Lyttleton, Lord G. *A History of the Life of King Henry II.* London: Sadby and Dodsley, 1767.
Of contemporary value only for the appended list of Norman participants at the pre-Hastings conference.

Maitland, Frederick William. *Domesday Book and Beyond: Three Essays in the Early History of England.* Cambridge: University Press, 1897. (Paperback: The Norton Library, 1966).
Still one of the best treatments of English society in the time of William the Conqueror and his sons.

Morris, W.A. "A Mention of Scutage in the Year 1100," *English Historical Review,* XXXVI (1921), pp. 45–46.
A rarely seen type of article, which introduces a new and important document into the field of medieval institutional history.

Norgate, Kate. *England Under the Angevin Kings.* 2 vols. London: Macmillan & Co., 1887.
An extremely detailed and important exposition of England in the period 1100 to 1216.

Oman, C.W.C. *The Art of War in the Middle Ages, A.D. 378–1515.* ed. J. Beeler. New York: Great Seal, 1953.
This revised edition of Oman's undergraduate essay of 1884 contains the essence, in generalized form, of his later and more famous volumes on medieval military history, including the discredited theory of the Middle Ages as cavalry-ridden and devoid of tactics and strategy.

Painter, Sidney. *Studies in the History of the English Feudal Barony.* Baltimore: Johns Hopkins Press, 1943.
An important study of the composition and problems of the English nobles during the period of this study.

Petit-Dutaillis, Charles. *The Feudal Monarchy in France and England in the Twelfth and Thirteenth Centuries.* trans. E. D. Hunt. London: Routledge and Kegan Paul, reprint 1964. (Paperback: Harper Torchbook).
A comparison of the development of royal power in the two leading medieval kingdoms.

Pirenne, Henri. *Histoire de Belgique.* 3 vols. Brussels: Lamertin, 1909.
Remains the most comprehensive history of the Low Countries by a master historian.

Pollock, F., and Maitland, F.W. *The History of English Law.* 2 vols., 2nd. ed. Cambridge: University Press, 1952.
A definitive guide to the intricacies of feudal legal development.

Poole, A.L. *Obligations of Society in the Twelfth and Thirteenth Centuries.* Oxford: Clarendon Press, 1946.
A short but significant volume which illustrates with authority the

transition in medieval England from an economy based on personal service to one based on money.

———. *From Domesday Book to Magna Carta, 1087–1216.* Oxford: Clarendon Press, 1951 (2nd. ed. 1955).
A comprehensive combination of monographic literature and original research into the twelfth century marks this entry in the Oxford History of England series.

Postan, M.M. "The Rise of the Money Economy," *Economic History Review,* XIV (1944), pp. 123–34.
A general discussion of the conditions which facilitated the hire of mercenaries.

Powicke, Michael. *Military Obligation in Medieval England: A Study in Liberty and Duty.* Oxford: Clarendon Press, 1962.
Although the main thrust of this work is directed toward obligatory military duty, and therefore concentrates on conscription and the fyrd, some note is made of the role played by mercenaries in the twelfth century.

Prestwich, J.O. "War and Finance in the Anglo-Norman State," *Transactions of the Royal Historical Society,* 5th series, IV (1954), pp. 19–43.
A pioneer work in the relationship between the rising money economy and the use of mercenaries in the Anglo-Norman period by the one author who has concentrated on mercenaries.

Ramsay, Sir. James H. *The Angevin Empire in the Three Reigns of Henry II, Richard I and John (AD 1154–1216).* London: S. Sonnenschein & Co., 1903.
Probably the most detailed account of twelfth-century England.

———. *A History of the Revenues of the Kings of England, 1066–1399.* Oxford: Clarendon Press, 1925.
Includes valuable detailed financial information relating to the economic potentiality of English monarchs to hire soldiers.

Richardson, H.G. and Sayles, G.O. *The Governance of Mediaeval England from the Conquest to the Magna Carta.* Edinburgh: University Press, 1963.
The most provocative recent book to appear on feudalism. Although the authors rightly downgrade feudalism and upgrade mercenaries, the support they bring to their position is unconvincing.

Rössler, Oskar. *Kaiserin Matilde.* Berlin: Ebering, 1897.
A standard, important biography of the Empress which treats her more sympathetically than is done elsewhere.

Round, John Horace. *Feudal England.* London: S. Sonnenschein & Co., 1909. (Reprint: London: G. Allen and Unwin, 1964).
The essay "Introduction of Knight Service into England," is a watershed in the historiography of the Norman Conquest and English medieval military institutions.

———. *Geoffrey de Mandeville: A Study in Anarchy.* London: Longmans, Green & Co., 1892. (Reprint: Burt Franklin).
A detailed study of the reign of Stephen which illustrates the tenuousness of the lord-vassal relationship.

Sayles, G.O. *The Medieval Foundations of England.* London: Methuen & Co., 1956.
Attacks Round's thesis of the Norman Conquest as cataclysmic by stressing continuity before and after 1066.

Stenton, F.M. *The First Century of English Feudalism, 1066–1166.* 2nd. ed. Oxford: Clarendon Press, 1961.
As the dates imply, this is a further explication of the Round thesis. Revisionists, of course, prefer to consider this period, from many aspects, the last *century of English feudalism.*

Stephenson, Carl. "Feudalism and its Antecedents in England," *American Historical Review,* XLVIII (1943), pp. 245–65.
Essentially a defense of the newness of the Norman contribution to England, developed by explaining away its antecedents.

Strayer, Joseph R. *Feudalism.* Princeton: Van Nostrand Co., 1965.
A deceptively short treatment of feudalism almost every sentence of which, like the Dictatus Papae *of Gregory VII, could well serve as the heading of a chapter. Contains key documents of feudalism, many translated by the author for the first time.*

Stubbs, William. *The Constitutional History of England.* 3 vols. Oxford: Clarendon Press, 1897.
A classic which the student of medieval institutions can ignore only at his own risk.

Varenbergh, Emile. *Histoire des relations diplomatiques entre le comte de Flandre et l'Angleterre.* Brussels: C. Muquardt, 1874.
Presents additional background information for the money fief and the use of Flemings as mercenaries by English kings.

Index

Abbotsbury, Abbot of, 56
aid, feudal, 25
Alan of Dinant, 47, 49
Alan of Richmond, 16
Alençon, battle of (1118), 39
Angoulême, 64, 65
Anjou, 28, 33, 34, 56, 57, 61, 62; money of, 57
Aquitaine 57, 63–65
Aragonese, 15
archers, 37, 45, 46, 48, 56, 65
architecture, Gothic, 5
armada (1173), 71
Arnulph of Montgomery, 38
Arques, 62
array, feudal, 9, 41
Arundel (castle), 38
Assize of Arms (1181), 67

Baldwin VII, count of Flanders, 39
Baldwin of Hainault, 43
Baldwin of Redwers, 44–45
Bampton, siege of (1142), 50
Basques, 15
Bayeux, bishop of, see Odo, b. of Bayeux
Becket, Thomas, 60
Bedfordshire, 42
Beowulf, 23
Bertrand of Born, 64
Berwick, 68
Berwyn (Wales), 59
Bolsover (castle), 70
Boulogne, 41–42; see also Eustace, c. of Boulogne, Matthew, c. of Boulogne
Brabant, 55
Brabantines, 15, 65
Bretons, 30
Bridgnorth (castle), 17, 38
Bristol, 50

Brittany, 28–29, 33, 61–62
Buckinghamshire, 57
Bungay (castle), 70
Bures (castle), 39
Burgundy, 29
Bury St. Edmund, 68

Caen, 29
Cambridge (castle), 70
Cambridgeshire, 42
Canterbury, 36, 48; see also Lanfranc, archb. of Canterbury
capitalism, 4, 5
captains, ship, 25, 71
Carlisle, 64
Cartae Baronum (1166), 9, 18, 22, 25
castle-guard, 25, 69, 70
chancellery, 40
Chaumont-sur-Loire (castle), 58–59
Chester, 48, 69; see also Ranulph, e. of Chester
Chinon (castle), 56
Church, lands of, 47, 74; revenues of, 40, 54
Circencester, siege of (1142), 50
Clito, William, see William Clito
Clun (castle), 69
Clwyd Valley (Wales), 58
Colchester (castle), 70
comitatus, 18
commutation, see scutage
Conquest, Norman, see Norman Conquest
Cornwall, 48; see also Reginald, e. of Cornwall
coterels, 15, 65
Courbaran, 65
Couronne, abbey of, 64
Coutances, bishop of, see Geoffrey, b. of Coutances
courts, royal, 53

crossbowmen, 32, 37, 48
Crusade, First, 37, 47

Dangeld, 43
David, king of the Scots, 46
Dermot McMurrough, 60
Devizes (castle), 47
Devonshire, 44, 48, 57
Dol (Brittany), 62
Domesday Survey (1086), 29, 31
Domfront, 15
Dorsetshire, 48
Dublin, 60
Durham, bishop of, *see* Ranulph Flambard, b. of Durham

East Anglia, 68
Elias, count of Maine, 37
Ely, 50; *see also* Nigel, b. of Ely
engineers, 25, 32, 37–38
Essex, 42
Eu, count of, *see* Robert, c. of Eu, William Busac of Eu
Eustace, count of Boulogne, 35, 38, 42
Eustace, son of Stephen, 42
Exchequer, 4, 11–12, 13, 39, 40, 53, 63, 74
Exeter (castle), 44–45
Eye, honor of, 41–42

feudalism, 3, 6, 7, 10, 12
fiefs, 22
fief-rentiers, 18, 19
Flambard, Ranulph, *see* Ranulph Flambard, b. of Durham
Flanders, 15, 29, 54, 62; civil wars in, 44; count of, 61; *see also* Baldwin VII, c. of Flanders, Robert II, c. of Flanders; flood (1110), 15
Flemings, 15, 29, 30
foot soldiers, 46, 65
Framlingham (castle), 68, 70
Freeman, Edward A., 67
fyrd, 60, 66, 67

Galway, Great Scutage of, *see* scutage
Gascony, 57, 64
Geoffrey of Anjou, 46
Geoffrey Boterel, 16
Geoffrey of Brittany, 28, 56
Geoffrey, bishop of Coutances, 35, 37

Geoffrey of Mandeville, 31, 50
Geoffrey Martel, 26
Gisors, 59
Gloucestershire, 48, 56; earl of, *see* Robert, e. of Gloucester
Gothic architecture, *see* architecture, Gothic
Grandmont, abbey of, 64
Gregory VII (pope), 34
Grosmont (castle), 69
guard, castle, *see* castle-guard
guerrilla warfare, 50, 56
Guy of Burgundy, 27

Hampshire, 42, 58
Harold, king of England, 26, 30
Hastings, 36, 70; battle of, 18, 30–31, 33
Henry I, king of England, 12, 15, 17, 19, 22, 23, 28, 39–43, 73
Henry II, king of England, 11, 12, 21, 24–25, 39, 41, 53–71, 72, 74; as duke of Normandy, 17, 51
Henry I, king of France, 26–27
Henry of Huntingdon, 29
Henry, bishop of Winchester, 17, 42, 49–50
Henry, the young king, 41, 61, 64
Hereford, 35, 48, 56, 57, 64, 69; earl of, *see* Roger, e. of Hereford
Hereward, 17
Hertford (castle), 70
Hertfordshire, 42
homage, 23
housecarles, Anglo-Saxon, 18
Hugh Bigod, 44, 68
Hugh Capet, 28
Hugh of Puiset, 17
Hugh of Montgomery, 37
Hugh, earl of Norfolk, 17
Huntingdon, 42, 48; *see also* Henry of Huntingdon

Ile de France, 28, 29
invasion, Anglo-Saxon of England, 6; by Curthose (1094), 36–37; Danish of England, 6, 34; Flemish, 34; Scottish, 44; Welsh, 44
Ireland, 61; expeditions to: (1171–72), 60–63; (1186–87), 64, 66, 72
Italy, 29, 75

John fitz Gilbert, 18
John, king of England, 20, 41
John the Marshal, 50
jury system, 4, 5
justices, travelling, 53

Kenilworth (castle), 70
Kent, 14, 35, 42, 49, 54, 57
knights'-fees, fragmentation of, 22
knight-service, 6, 10, 12, 21, 23, 52, 66, 69, 75; annual length of, 20, 45, 54; death blow to, 24

LaMarche, 65
Lancaster, 41, 42
Lanfranc, archbishop of Canterbury, 32; death of, 36
Lateran Council (1137), 48
Leicester (castle), 67; county of, 68; earl of, *see* Robert, e of Leicester; "Leicester War," 68
LeMans, 38, 65
Lillebonne, 29
Lincoln, 42, 47, 49
Limoges, 64
Limousin, 64, 65
London, 57, 61
Loo, abbey of St. Peter at, *see* St. Peter at Loo
Loudon (castle), 56
Louis VII, king of France, 59, 63
Lupatius, 65

Machiavelli, Niccolo, 75, 76
Maine, 20, 29, 33, 37, 56, 61, 62; count of, *see* Elias, c. of Maine
Matilda, Empress, 15, 24, 41ff; arrives in England (1139), 48; departs England (1148), 48
Matilda, wife of Stephen, 42, 49
Matthew of Boulogne, 41, 61, 62
Mercadier, 65
Mercenaries, arrows for, 58; battle axes for, 58; Brabantine, 62, 63; Breton, 15, 37, 39, 74-75; Burgundian, 37; class characteristics, 16; Danish, 58; Flemish, 17, 37, 43, 50, 52, 54, 55, 58, 65, 68, 72, 74-75; French, 37; garments for, 61; Gascon, 66; greed of, 16; hired by barons, 17; naval, 71; professional-

Mercenaries (*Cont.*)
ism of, 16, 17; quartered in England, 34; salaries for, 58; shields for, 58; transportation of, 58-59; uniforms for, 58; (1139-49), 44; Welsh, 38-39, 57, 59, 62-65, 71, 75
Middlesex, 56
milites solidarii, 66
militia, 19, 55, 57, 60, 66, 67, 68; *see also* fyrd
miners, 45
Mirabeau (castle), 56
money fief, 19, 21
Mont St. Michel, 15, 20
Mortain, 33, 41, 42; *see also* Robert, c. of Mortain, William, c. of Mortain
"muster roll" (1166), 9-10

Newcastle-on-Tyne (castle), 70
Newcastle-under-Lyme (castle), 70
New Monarchies, 75
Nigel, bishop of Ely, 17, 47
Norfolk, 35, 42, 44, 48, 49, 57; *see also* Hugh, e. of Norfolk, Ralph, e. of Norfolk
Norman Conquest, 6, 18, 21, 26, 28, 31
Normandy, 20, 33, 35, 57, 58; fiscal organization of, 27-28; *see also* Richard II, d. of Normandy, William the Conqueror, as d. of Normandy
Northallerton, battle of, 46
Northampton, 48, 58, 70
Northumberland, 15, 48; *see also* Robert Mowbray, e. of Northumberland
Norwich (castle), 32, 44, 70
Nottingham (castle), 70; county, 42

Odo, bishop of Bayeux, 29, 33, 35
Orderic Vitalis, 30
Oswestry, 59, 69, 70
Owen, 56
Oxford, 42, 49, 50, 70; siege of (1142), 50

Paris, 62, 63
Peace of God, 47-48
Peak (castle), 70
Pembrokeshire, 15, 54, 60, 61; *see also* Richard, e. of Pembroke
Perigord, 65

Peterborough, abbot of, *see* Turold, a. of Peterborough
Philip of Flanders, 61
Philip II Augustus, king of France, 37, 65
Pipe Rolls, 40, 55, 69; (1130), 12, 22, 42-43; (1159), 57; (1161-62), 58, 62; (1173-74), 69; (1186-87), 64
Poitiers, 63
Poitou, 29, 62-65
Porchester (castle), 70
Prudhoe (castle), 70
Pyrenees, 64

quotas, for knight-service, 6-8

Radcot, siege of (1142), 50
Ralph of Fougères, 62
Ralph (of Gael), earl of Norfolk and Suffolk, 31-33
Ralph the Staller, 31
Ranulph, earl of Chester, 71
Ranulph Flambard, bishop of Durham, 36-38
Raymond of Brun, 64
recruitment, 10
Reginald, earl of Cornwall, 17
retainers, household, 18-19, 21
revolts, 73; (1047), 27; (1052), 27; (1075), 31; (1078), 32-33; (1082), 33; (1088), 35-36; (1095), 37; (1101-1102), 17, 38, 42, 74; (1173-74), 55, 61, 67-69
Rhuddlan (Wales), 58
Richard of Bienfaite, 32
Richard of Clare, earl of Striguil, *see* "Strongbow"
Richard the Lion-Hearted, 41, 62-65
Richard of Lucy, 67-68
Richard fitz Nigel, 11
Richard II, duke of Normandy, 28
Richard, earl of Pembroke, 62
Robert of Bellême, 17, 33, 35-36, 38, 42
Robert Curthose, 33, 35, 37-38, 72-73
Robert, count of Eu, 29
Robert II, count of Flanders, 19
Robert the Frisian, 15
Robert, earl of Gloucester, 45-46, 49-50, 72
Robert of Lacy, 38
Robert, earl of Leicester, 17, 68

Robert Malet, 42
Robert, count of Mortain, 29, 35, 41
Robert Mowbray, earl of Northumberland, 37
Robert of Torigni, 56
Rochester, 35
Roger of Beaumont, 29
Roger, earl of Hereford, 31-33
Roger of Lacy, 37
Roger of Montgomery, 29, 33, 35, 37-39, 42
Roger, bishop of Salisbury, 47
Roland (Irish rebel), 64
Roses, War of the, *see* War of the Roses
Rouen, archbishop of, 27; siege of, 61-63
Round, John Horace, 6-9, 32
routiers, 15
ruta, 15
Ruthin (castle), 69

Sailors, 58, 71
St. Martial, abbey of, 64
St. Peter at Loo, abbey of, 54
Saintes, 62-63
Saintonge, 64
Salisbury (castle), 70; *see also* Roger, b. of Salisbury
Sancho of Saragnac, 65
Sandwich, Isle of, 71
Scots, king of, *see* David, k. of the Scots
scutage, 13, 22, 23, 36, 37, 39, 40, 46, 54-57, 63, 66, 71, 74; (1130), 22; (1161-62), 58; (1171-72), 60; (1186-87: Great Scutage of Galway), 64; collected by Robert of Gloucester, 50
sergeants, 14
sheriff, 25, 31, 53, 55, 67
Shrawardine (castle), 69
Shrewsbury (castle), 38, 58; *see also* Robert of Bellême, e. of Shrewsbury
Shropshire, 56, 58, 64, 69
Skenfrith (castle), 69
slingers, 45
snipers (Welsh), 59
solidarii, 14; *milites solidarii*, 66
Somerset, 35, 42, 48
Southampton, 45, 58

Standard, battle of, 43, 46
Stephen, king of England, 12, 14–17, 19–20, 24, 30, 39, 40–52, 54, 72, 74
stipendiarii, 14
strategy, medieval, 10, 11
Striguil, earl of, Richard of Clare, *see* "Strongbow"
"Strongbow," 60, 63
Stubbs, Bishop, 55, 66, 67
subinfeudation, 7–9, 22, 24
Suffolk, 42, 44, 48, 49, 57; *see also* Ralph, e. of Suffolk
Surrey, 42
Sussex, 35

tactics, medieval, 10–11
Taillebourg (castle), 64
tax, income, 4
Thames Valley, 49
thegns, Anglo-Saxon, 7, 18
Thierry of Alsace, 15, 43, 44
Tickhill (castle), 38
Tinchebrai, battle of (1106), 39, 41
Torigni, Robert of, *see* Robert of Torigni
Toulouse, campaign to, 57–58, 65
Touraine, 56, 61
tournament, 11
travelling justices, *see* justices, travelling
Truce of God, 47–48
Turold, abbot of Peterborough, 17

university, 4

Val-es-Dunes, battle of, 27
Verneuil, siege of, 61–62
Vexin, 37
vicomtes, 28

Wales, 19, 55, 57–58, 69, 72; expeditions to: (1157), 56; (1165), 58, 61, 65, 66

Wallingford, 56
Walter Giffard, 29
War of the Roses, 24
Wareham, siege of (1142), 50
Wark-on-Tweed (castle), 70
Warwick (castle), 70
Waterford (Ireland), 60
Wiglaf, 23
William fitz Alan, 69
William of Arques, 27
William of Breteuil, 33
William Busac of Eu, 27
William of Cambresis, 65
William Clito, 39
William the Conqueror, 5–7, 13, 18, 20, 23, 26, 32, 33, 40–41, 72–73; as duke of Normandy, 26–27
William Cumin, 56
William of Dover, 16
William the Lion, king of the Scots, 67–68
William, count of Mortain, 27
William of Newburgh, 63
William fits Osbern, 29, 31, 33
William Rufus, 13, 17, 19, 34, 72, 73
William, son of Stephen, 41
William of Warrenne, 31, 32, 38
William of Ypres, 14–17, 43–45, 47, 49–50, 52, 54, 72
Winchester, 49, 54; siege of (1141), 49–50, 72; treaty of (1153), 51; *see also* Henry, b. of Winchester
White Castle, 69–70
Whittington (castle), 69
Wight, Isle of, 45
Wilton, 50
Wiltshire, 48
Windsor (castle), 70
Worcester, 35, 70; *see also* Wulfstan, b. of Worcester
writs of admission, 25
Wulfstan, bishop of Worcester, 19, 35

STUDIES IN BRITISH HISTORY AND CULTURE

DATE DUE

4/17

MAY 21 1975			
GAYLORD			PRINTED IN U.S.A.